Cardinal Virtues
IN FOCUS

Dear Rusty,

Holiness is built on
human virtues. A token of
appreciation, may this book
inspire you in your
spiritual journey.
God Bless!

Fr Henry B.

Cardinal Virtues
IN FOCUS

Why It Matters to Think & Act Well

HENRY BOCALA

Scepter

Published by Scepter Publishers, Inc.
info@scepterpublishers.org
www.scepterpublishers.org
800-322-8773
New York

Cover design by StudioRed Design
Page design and pagination by Rose Design

Library of Congress Control Number: 2021947553

ISBN (pbk): 9781594174421
ISBN (eBook): 9781594174438

Printed in the United States of America

CONTENTS

ACKNOWLEDGMENTS

"No man is an island," wrote the English poet John Donne (1572–1631). Nobody is self-sufficient; everyone relies on others. This proverb holds true in relation to this book. *Cardinal Virtues in Focus* would not have been possible without the support of many people.

First of all, I sincerely thank Larry Olsen and Fr. Joseph Keefe, who encouraged me to write the book, reviewed the manuscript, and gave valuable input. I am grateful, too, to David Gallagher for allowing me to use his unpublished article on the perfect form of justice in St. Thomas Aquinas. The late Fr. James Albrecht also deserves credit for providing me with useful bibliography and reference materials.

Good ideas hardly bear fruit unless they are published and spread. On the technical side, this book finally saw the light of day, thanks to Scepter Publishers. In particular, I would like to express my heartfelt gratitude to Robert Singerline, John Powers, Meredith Koopman, and the whole editorial and production teams for their professional expertise and excellent work.

Finally, I am deeply indebted to Rev. Msgr. Fernando Ocáriz, the Prelate of Opus Dei, and all my former professors at the Faculty of Theology at the University of Navarre (Pamplona, Spain) and the Faculty of Canon Law at the Pontifical University of the Holy Cross (Rome, Italy). They have played a big role in my spiritual and intellectual formation and deserve to be acknowledged for any good this book might bring to souls.

INTRODUCTION

ardinal Virtues in Focus: Why It Matters to Think and Act Well. Another book on virtues that nobody reads and ends up stacked on the bookshelf? This question popped into my head as I was toying with the idea of writing this book. Yet, time and again, we need to re-invent ourselves, and people are looking for new ways to revisit the ABCs of a good and righteous life.

This book is not your typical feel-good, self-help paperback or collection of "chicken soup" (cure-all) stories. Rather, it offers a blend of moral principles and practical tips, age-old wisdom with down-to-earth examples that lead the reader to the fundamentals of a virtuous life.

Every person as he or she happens to be is distinct from the person as he or she should be.[1] Since we often fall short of our ideals in life, we still have a long way to go to reach the peak of moral maturity. Yet we desire to attain our full human potential, our inherent purpose or *raison d'être* (reason for existence). Morality is *teleological* (Greek *telos*: end, purpose, goal). In his *Nicomachean Ethics*, Aristotle said our character is determined not by what we think is good or evil, but by our choice of good or evil.[2] This requires moral excellence, the practice of human virtues.

What is a moral virtue in the first place? It is a firm attitude and stable disposition to do the good, allowing us not only to do what is right but also to give the best of ourselves. Virtues are habitual perfections of intellect and will that govern our actions and passions so that we do not fall into excesses or defects.[3] A person acquires human virtues by reason of repeating good acts until good habits are formed. And habits—good or bad—tend to persist, as expressed by the English idiom, "Old habits die hard."

In the boys' school where I used to work as a chaplain, a third-grade teacher had a clever idea of sending "happy notes" to parents each time their child behaved especially well in class. Printed on the note cards was: *Gotcha! I was caught being* "a good friend," "kind with my words," or "responsible," with a little tick box next to each positive behavior. Below it read: *Please celebrate with your child tonight.*

The "happy notes" did reinforce good conduct and helped the boys—who were chosen beforehand—to become even better. But virtues are not just for children. Rooted in human nature, virtues imply manliness (from the Latin *virtus, vir*— man, and *vis*—power). They are operative habits by which a person uses all his or her faculties to seek the good. A righteous man or woman is not at the mercy of disordered impulses but acts according to principles, thanks to his or her self-dominion and right use of freedom.

Moral life is not all about fulfilling norms and external rules in a classic form of voluntarism, as if we had to prove our capacity to be good by sheer willpower. We become virtuous not by opposing our inclinations or getting rid of our feelings, but by developing our character with a positive outlook in life. The key is formation of the intellect, the will, and the passions, so that we become persons of integrity. Ideas are clear, sentiments are well ordered, and the heart expands, along with the capacity to serve others and rejoice in the good.[4]

Do moral virtues still matter today? Are rules of conduct relevant in contemporary society? Virtues are eminently personal, but they have great social repercussions. Criminality, juvenile delinquency, fraudulence, suicide, and the like are not merely offshoots of structural defects of a body politic. They're bred by personal vices, individuals' lack of virtues. Professional ethics are essential in the fields of law, business, medicine, journalism, education, and politics. Work, family, romance, and friendship thrive on respect, kindness, honesty, order, and so forth. If you drop by your favorite bookstore, you'll find a host of best-selling titles that reveal the "Secrets of a Happy Marriage," "Habits of a Successful Entrepreneur," or "The Art of Effective Leadership." Well, they're all about human virtues, written in a popular style.

We often make important decisions in life, so we need to think and act well, discerning the proper course of action in every instance. That's *prudence*. Every day we interact with people who possess rights and deserve respect just as we do, so we had better be fair and considerate with others. That's *justice*. Difficulties can hold us back from pursuing our goals, so we must have inner strength to conquer our fears and embrace challenge. That's *fortitude*. Sometimes, base appetites get the better of us and we exceed proper limits, so we must curb our desires and moderate our impulses. That's *temperance*.

These are the four cardinal virtues (from Latin *cardo*—hinge), so-called because they are primary qualities required for upright life and all the other human virtues hinge on them. This grouping from antiquity facilitates true interior freedom. The Book of Wisdom in the Old Testament states: "And if any one loves righteousness, her labors are virtues; for she teaches self-control and prudence, justice and courage; nothing in life is more profitable for men than these" (Wis 8:7).

The cardinal virtues are specific virtues with different formal objects that imply distinct habits.[5] In reality, however, they are so deeply intertwined that none of them truly exists without the other three. Hence, no prudence is genuine unless one is just, courageous, and temperate; no temperance is perfect unless one is brave, just, and prudent; and so forth.

In this book, a chapter is devoted to each of the cardinal virtues, following the structure developed by St. Thomas Aquinas in his *Summa Theologica*: notion of the virtue, contrary vices, and the three parts of a virtue: integral, subjective, and potential. The *integral parts* are elements that must be present for any perfect act of a virtue. For example, there is no *prudent* act without *foresight*. The *subjective parts* are related to a cardinal virtue as the species of a genus are related to the genus. Thus, justice has for its subjective parts commutative justice (relation between individuals) and distributive justice (relation of the state to its citizens). Finally, the *potential parts* of a cardinal virtue share something in common with it as the principal virtue but fall short of its perfection. *Perseverance* (steadfastness) is related to *fortitude* in this way.

It is my hope that whoever reads this book gains insights on the cardinal moral virtues and their related virtues, such as honesty, obedience, generosity, and humility. Virtues, though, are not meant only to be appreciated, but to be lived. In *The Book of Virtues*, author William Bennett says that we talk of values and how important it is to have them, as if they were beads on a string or marbles in a pouch. In a sense, "virtues are not something to have," he adds, "but are something to be, the most important thing to be, as part of human nature."[6] Virtue implies personal change, inner transformation.

Our own experience tells us that human virtues are not always easy to practice. We bear witness to how hard it is to control our temper, be totally sincere, fulfill our duties, or stay calm in the face of adversities. But virtues are not impossible. Despite human frailties, every person has a radical capacity to be good. Yes, we will never be perfect, but it doesn't matter. What's important is that we are earnest, we start again and again, and we don't give up the fight. Virtues are not acquired overnight; developing good habits is a lifelong task.

But there is good news. Believers in Christ—and he invites absolutely everyone to believe in him (Jn 3:15; Mk 16:16)—can count on the help of the infused moral virtues which are bestowed upon us by God, not cultivated by our own efforts. Unlike their corresponding natural virtues, the infused or supernatural moral virtues are not only guided by reason but also illumined by faith. Aquinas heavily relied on Aristotle to develop his fourfold system of cardinal virtues, but the Angelic Doctor went far beyond the Greek philosopher. Aristotle did not have Christian revelation, and so his vision was confined to rational living, human plenitude, equilibrium of soul, personal growth, and natural happiness.

But Christians believe that the ultimate purpose of human life is union with God. We are called, as it were, not just to be a "good man" or a "good woman," but to be nothing less than saints. Everyone is destined for supernatural happiness, and this entails participation in the divine life. No amount of acquired virtue will make us capable of attaining beatitude. Yet the baptized Christian is transformed by God's grace and is aided by the infused moral virtues of prudence, justice, fortitude, and temperance, along with the theological virtues of faith, hope, and charity, and the gifts of the Holy Spirit. What we can't reach as creatures on the natural plane, we can attain on the supernatural plane with the infused virtues that enable us to act in a way befitting a child of God.[7]

Thus, in every chapter of this book the exposition of a cardinal virtue concludes with a short section on the corresponding infused moral virtue (that is, Christian prudence, justice, fortitude, and temperance). Nevertheless, grace does not destroy but builds on nature. God's assistance doesn't mean we no longer have to work, for he helps most especially those who help themselves. The presence of infused fortitude or temperance in the life of a Christian doesn't mean he or she uses it well or even at all. It simply means that the person need not rely merely on his or her own feeble strength, thanks to the aid of grace and the role of the Paraclete.[8] And that's an infinite help.

"Finally, brethren, whatever is true, whatever is honorable, whatever is just, whatever is pure, whatever is lovely, whatever is gracious, if there is any excellence, if there is anything worthy of praise, think about these things" (Phil 4:8).

CHAPTER 1

The Virtue of Prudence

Have you ever made an important decision in life, only to regret it terribly later on? At that moment, you were so sure of yourself, so convinced that it was the best thing to do, that you simply brushed off words of caution from a friend or the advice of your mom and dad. But one day, you had a deep realization that proved them right! How you wish you could rewind time and start all over again! For then, you would be wiser. If only you had thought the decision through better the first time around!

Human life is like a chess game. It offers well-nigh infinite possibilities on which we need to decide. Every choice we make matters, every decision has consequences down the line. It is important to have foresight and weigh our options carefully. Once we know what to do, we must act right away. Mistakes can happen, but we learn from them. The best move is not random, but well planned.

What a good player does in a chess game, the virtue of prudence does in our life, *mutatis mutandis*.[1] Just as he finds the best move and executes it, so too, prudence determines the best course of action and carries it out. Prudence is the ability to make right choices and act well in every instance. The virtue implies intellectual traits like judgment, memory, foresight, and caution, all of which help us make wise decisions.

Real life of course is not a game of chess; it is a lot more complex and the stakes are infinitely higher. Besides, we are not like a pawn, treated as expendable, valued the least, manipulated and shoved around. As a person, we hate being always told what to do, whether by our parents, teacher, boss, or spouse. We highly prize independence. Being in control of what goes on in our life gives us a sense of fulfillment.

Free and Autonomous

Every human person is an autonomous and self-determining individual.[2] Created in the *image and likeness of God*,[3] we are rational beings who possess freedom and interior space proper to human dignity. Being able to act freely gives us depth and identity. But we must nurture and safeguard that innermost sphere if we want to develop self-mastery.[4]

We are born free, yet not everyone knows how to use well his freedom, which is the power, rooted in reason and will, to do this or that, and so to act on our own responsibility. Freedom is a force of growth and maturity in truth and goodness.[5] But this capacity to act has its inherent risks, the tendency of man in his fallen nature to abuse freedom and fall into error.

Some time ago, I had a dinner with a long-lost friend who claimed to be a "free thinker." Aware that I was teaching an ethics class, he asked me, "Why doesn't God remove evil from our lives?" We met for a relaxed get-together, not a roundtable discussion, so I just told him that "the only real evil is sin, and it's the result of the misuse of freedom. God can't take away our freedom, or rather, he can but he won't, because then we would cease to be human." That short chat eventually led him back to the Faith.

I mention this story because prudence is nothing other than the correct use of human freedom. Life is both a gift and a project. Every individual is unfinished. We are in the state of becoming, day and night. The Book of Sirach in the Old Testament says that from the beginning, God created man and "left him in the power of his own inclination" (Sir 15:14). We are thus the protagonist of our own life.[6]

But do we always do the right thing? How come people make bad choices? Poor judgments? Stupid decisions? Terrible mistakes? Sometimes, confronted with a problem, we just do not know what to do or how to resolve it. Or maybe we do know, but in the end still fail to act well.

Right Reason in Action

The virtue of prudence enables us to form sound judgments and act wisely. Prudence, in a nutshell, is right reason in action (*recta ratio agibilium*). In his *Nicomachean Ethics*, the Greek philosopher Aristotle defines prudence as the virtue by which we grasp the truth, using reason to discern what is good in leading a virtuous and happy life (Greek *eudaimonia*).[7] In other words, a prudent person knows the right thing to do at each moment. St. Thomas Aquinas echoes Aristotle's notion of prudence and defines it succinctly as "wisdom concerning human affairs."[8]

First of all, prudence is an intellectual virtue, the habit to reason well and think right. It perfects our understanding, puts order in our thoughts, guides our emotions, and directs our conduct. Prudence sets the mean of reason in human behavior, helping us determine the best course of action here and now. If someone tells you, "Hey, you did the right thing. That was a good call, man!" what he is saying is that you made a prudent decision.

However, prudence is also a moral virtue since it leads to action. It is at once sound judgment and character excellence, correct reasoning and good habits. Prudence is not theoretical but practical knowledge, knowledge that leads us to behave well. Knowledge of itself has little use unless it is properly applied. We would not consult a doctor who acquired his medical knowledge just from the textbooks, with zero practical training. Similarly, it is through hands-on experience that the virtue of prudence is cultivated. No wonder prudence is aptly called practical wisdom or street-smart virtue.

Human acts are concrete and down-to-earth. They are interwoven into life's circumstances, which vary a great deal. Problems in our family, business, studies, health, or work can pose a moral dilemma. "Why can't I make up my mind?" "What am I supposed to do in this case?" There is no code of conduct listing all the dos and don'ts in life, like a product operation manual. We thus need a tool to point out the fair means, the right balance that applies general principles to a particular case. That is where prudence can guide our decision-making, helping us develop insights, overcome doubts, avoid pitfalls, and reach our good end. St. Augustine wrote that prudence is essentially love discerning aright that which helps from that which hinders us in tending to God.[9]

Acquired Virtue

Life is a series of choices. Once we reach the age of reason, we begin to use our freedom non-stop in manifold situations. That covers practically all our waking hours. In a sense, we are who we choose to be. Nobody really answers for the kind of person we become except we ourselves.[10] We shape our life and mold our own character. The films we opt to watch, the friends we spend time with, the places we hang out, the books we pick to read, the websites we click on, the food we eat, the career we pursue, the woman or man we marry, and the state of life we embrace—all these choices transform us to become who we are. Since life offers a wide range of possibilities, we had better know how to choose and act well. This requires a good blend of learning and experience.

Children cannot be called prudent for an obvious reason: they lack maturity. The perfected ability to make right decisions requires time. Natural prudence implies acts and experience and so it cannot be found in children, says Aquinas.[11] Little boys and girls have yet to be initiated in rational thinking, in the school of virtues. They tend to act by puerile instinct; their notion of right and wrong is mostly fed by Mom and Dad. Children are expected to obey because they cannot make decisions for themselves. In every new situation they encounter, little kids need guidance.[12]

But when small children grow up they gradually enjoy a certain degree of independence; they own their actions more and more. Their parents need not always tell them what to do. Little by little, children face their inner world, alone with themselves, totally free, and capable of self-domination.[13] A unique personality unfolds that is partly shaped by their environment and partly bears the stamp of their conscious acts.

However, prudence does not automatically develop with age. It is acquired by way of effort and repetition of good acts. We are not surprised that some adults act childishly. If a person is not accustomed to doing the right thing, if he grows up making bad choices, we can hardly depend on him. On the other hand, many young people act quite maturely, thanks to their good upbringing and, for the baptized, the infused virtue of prudence.

Somehow prudence cannot be easily passed on to others. Prudent people live this virtue by force of habit and are barely able to explain how they make wise decisions. They train in the school of life itself. Quite naturally, they are sensible and far-sighted, never acting carelessly. As we grow up we get more experience in life, we understand a lot of things without anyone teaching us. This knowledge is partly innate, partly learned.

Auriga Virtutum

Prudence is the measure of moral virtues, since it provides a model of ethically good conduct. It enjoys a position of preeminence among the four cardinal virtues, for only a prudent person can see rightly and act accordingly in all life's circumstances.[14]

For this reason, classical Greek philosophers and Christian thinkers, notably Aquinas, considered prudence as the *auriga virtutum*—charioteer of the virtues. The metaphor could not be more apt. Being a charioteer is not a simple task. The charioteer must have a vision and purpose, know where he or she is going, understand the instincts of his or her horses, and be able to harness their energies, control their movements, and stop them from going certain ways.

Similarly, the virtue of prudence directs all the other virtues, pointing out their characteristic just means, so that they do not stray toward disordered extremes.[15] The first cardinal virtue is tasked, so to speak, to determine in each moment those circumstances of time, place, manner, and so forth, which must be observed, and which classical philosophers called *medium rationis* (mean of reason).

Consider these simple cases. Driving with your family on a long road trip can be fun and exciting. You are all set to go when you hear a forecast of severe weather with heavy snow and gusty winds. Is it wise to brave it and take the risk? Telling the truth is honesty and generally good, but would you share with your spouse highly classified information you know by reason of your work? You are diabetic but your granddaughter made a caramel ice cream for your birthday. Will you take a scoop or two or more, or none at all? In these cases, what makes our act virtuous or not is determined by prudence.

All virtues are necessarily prudent. Prudence and the morally good are basically one and the same. The two concepts are interchangeable. It permeates all virtues, and all virtues embody prudence. Every virtue is such because of its prudential character.[16] When we say that a person is prudent, we really mean that he practices all the virtues. If you mortify your curiosity by closing those sleazy internet pop-ups, you are practicing temperance. But it is also a prudent act. If you tell the truth even if you find it hard to do so, that is fortitude. But it is also a prudent move. If you work overtime to finish an urgent job you are paid to do, you are being fair and just. But it is also a measure of prudence.

Every sin is opposed to prudence. Whoever commits a sin is imprudent because of pride, lust, gluttony, wrath, greed, envy, or sloth. These are all excesses or defects, behaviors that are not regulated by a prudent mind. Thus, prudence is the cause, root, mother, measure, precept, guide, and prototype of all ethical virtues.

Virtue versus Technique

Robert Vanderpoel of the *Chicago Sun-Times* famously said that "the most successful businessman is the man who holds onto the old just as long as it is *good*, and grabs the new just as soon as it is better." It may be wise advice from the technical point of view, but not necessarily from the moral standpoint. A person may be *good* at managing business yet ignore ethics, just as an investor can be honest, but inept at running a business.[17]

Captains of ships passing through the Panama Canal are required to hand over the vessel to authorized pilots especially trained to maneuver through the narrow, intricate waterway. Certified pilots are *good* at navigating the canal. Yet again, expert pilotage through locks and gates concerns technical prudence more than moral virtue.

The distinction is important. Aristotle rightly said that an artisan or craftsman who does a lousy job knowingly is not as bad as the one who does it just as poorly but unwittingly. Not so in the realm of virtues. The man who knows that he is doing something morally bad is certainly worse than the one who is unaware of his error.[18]

As we can see, human activity can take two forms: moral action-doing (*agere*) and physical action-making (*facere*). On the one hand, the perfection of our ability to *do*, to carry out *deeds*, is called moral prudence (*recta ratio agibilium*). *Good deeds* (behavior, human conduct) lead to self-realization; they produce fine, virtuous people. On the other hand, the perfection of our ability to make, to fabricate *works*, is known as art or technique (*recta ratio factibilium*). *Good works* (production, manufacture) give rise to artifacts, inventions, masterpieces.[19]

Prudence gives opportune advice on points regarding the proper end of a certain endeavor. Thus, we can speak of a *prudent* or *good* army commander (a dependable military leader) and a *prudent* or *good* heart surgeon (a skillful cardio specialist). These people are *prudent* or *good* but only in a relative sense of the word. Theirs is an *imperfect prudence*, says Aquinas.[20] Only good acts that pertain to a person's whole life and his or her last end are morally *prudent*; only those that help human conduct attain the ultimate good can be considered *prudent* in the absolute sense of the word.[21]

The French philosopher Jacques Maritain (1882–1973) wrote that the very notion of *morals* is just that—it is a practical science whose aim is to procure humanity's unqualified good or absolute good. *Ethics* is not about the perfection of what a person does or the works he or she produces, but the perfection of the agent him- or herself, the use he or she freely makes of his or her faculties.[22]

Founts of Prudence

A morally good life is built on right decisions which in turn are formed from two sources: the knowledge of *universal principles* of reason and the *relevant singulars*. The former is none other than the natural conscience, known as *synderesis*.[23] The latter are important facts, concrete data, or contingent realities.

Synderesis is a natural habit which leads one to do good and shun evil.[24] It is a property of the soul that can never be lost, is never mistaken, and whose objects are the first principles of the moral order. These principles are self-evident; they do not need deliberation. Every person, regardless of creed and culture, is enjoined by his or her innate conscience: "Do good and avoid evil." Synderesis expresses the common, overriding goal of all human acts.[25]

In our daily life we scarcely think in philosophical terms, if at all. Yet synderesis is something that permeates all human actions. When a man goes into a rage, gives in to lust, shoplifts, or lies to his wife, deep down he knows that he commits a sin. He does not have to be told that he did something wrong. He knows it by way of *a priori* habitual knowledge we call synderesis. St. Jerome refers to it as *scintilla conscientiae*—the spark of conscience, through which we grasp the first moral precepts in a way that is simple, natural, immediate, and infallible.[26]

Knowledge of the first moral principles is crucial, but is not quite enough for us to make a prudent decision. The *when*, *where*, and *how* of a given situation must be factored in. We need to focus on the real world, people, things, and events. Faced with multiple options, a person must think things over and pick the suitable means before taking any action.

Here comes the tricky thing. The higher the level of abstraction on which we think, the more certitude we have. But as we come down to more specific moral precepts, combined with more particular circumstances, it gets harder to ascertain what is right and wrong. Concrete cases involve many variables that make the thought process more complex.[27] There may be gray areas that require careful discernment.

To illustrate this point, we do not need a doctorate in moral theology to know that murder, theft, rape, and perjury are evil deeds, for these involve higher moral principles. But things are not as simple when, for example, we deal with a high-risk pregnancy where the survival of the unborn baby poses a threat to the mother's life. A host of factors need to be taken into account to determine the right course of action. So too, is the case of a CEO who plans to lay off some workers to keep his or her company afloat in times of recession, or a judge who receives death threats amidst a criminal case he or she handles. In these situations, things do not appear black and white; one needs to figure out the best thing to do.

This does not mean that in a complex moral situation we cannot be objective and are thus forced to act based on gut feeling. We certainly can, but we need special intellectual aptitudes supplied by prudence, such as memory, foresight, counsel, docility, and caution.[28] Precisely, it is the role of prudence to apply general moral criteria to concrete cases and decide what to do. Loosely, we may call the virtue of prudence "situation conscience."[29]

Once we know things well, we can decide and act well. The truth—the moral principles and relevant facts—conditions our mind. People often fumble and stumble due to ignorance. Misinformed and bereft of an ethical compass, they are at the mercy of pressures both from without (fads, opinions, polls, and ideologies) and from within (pride, greed, lust, anger, gluttony, envy, and sloth). More than once I have overheard this remark: "Sorry for my mistake, but I acted in good faith anyway." Yes, but it is not enough to mean well. We must do the right thing as best we can.

In our frenetic world we are often busy, rushing here and there. Activism leaves little room for reflection. Decisions are made hastily. We act on the spur of the moment. Things are not weighed properly. It certainly helps to pause and ponder every now and then. Form the habit of deep thinking! "Prudence as cognition" of the concrete situation includes the ability to be still in order to attain an objective perception of reality.[30] St. Josemaría Escrivá advised us to "try to keep our peace, even if only so as to act intelligently, since the man who remains calm is able to think, to study the pros and cons, to examine judiciously the outcome of the actions he is about to undertake."[31]

Moreover, passions (for example, love, fear, sadness, hatred) can eclipse our mind and weaken our will, so we need to be clear-headed and firm when making a decision. Many of our errors are not exactly due to ignorance; we just lack self-control and so fall into excesses. In our fallen nature, a state marked by inner dishar-mony, by rebellion of passions against the intellect and the will, we are prone to moral aberration.[32] Passions need to be bridled to some extent so that they do not corrupt our good judgment, which is what happens when we do what we know we should not, or omit what we know we should do.[33]

Integral Parts

The integral parts of a virtue are the various elements that help it complete its operation. Every prudent act is built on the knowledge of realities, mostly daily events. Acquiring such knowledge requires a series of "mini virtues" that serve as parts of prudence, and these are needed so that the human act may be truly wise and prudent.

1. Memory

We need prudence to face the future, but we also need the past to be prudent. *Memory* is a starting point in decision-making. It helps to have a great deal of experience, which is a motley collec-tion of memories. Memory here is not a simple ability to recall hard facts, involving a technique or mnemonic device we may have used in high school to build our vocabulary. Past events are useful only if we are able to draw lessons from them. We also tend to recall things in a way colored by certain biases, so we end up with a distorted vision of reality. Then, there are events not worth remembering, like grudges, nostalgia, or bitterness that prevent us from moving on.

Memory implies openness to reality—what truly happened, not what I think happened or wish would have happened. What counts is a "true to being" memory[34] which is a receptacle of the truth of things.[35] We store truths, facts, and convictions to retrieve them at the opportune moment, much like opening old but useful files kept in an external hard drive. Only deep souls used to reflection are able to do this. "I knew it. I shouldn't have ignored it. How come I didn't think of it? This isn't the first time it happened to me." Do these lines sound familiar?

History is an open book. We can face what lies ahead better if we have a good grasp of what has gone before. Your biography is a sort of reference material that guides your next steps. Prudence requires that we recall where we made the wrong turn so as not to fall into the same pit again. Or where we succeeded so we can repeat the deed, if not do it better the second, third, or nth time around.

2. Understanding

Understanding implies knowledge of the first principles (synderesis) which we have just seen, and awareness of the present situation. While memory or experience is valuable, it is still a little too broad to guide our decisions. Something more is needed. Situations can vary a great deal and a little twist of circumstance can spell a big difference. We thus need to examine up close the here and now. A clear understanding of the present (*intellectus*) that is rooted in the first principles is another integral part of the virtue of prudence.[36] It is the ability to capture data that truly matter, information that has special significance. We need to be informed of what is happening now and assess the current situation.

The Greek philosopher Heraclitus (c. 535–c. 475 BC), famous for his notion of ever-present change (constant flux or becoming), once said that, "No man ever steps in the same river twice, for it is not the same river and he is not the same man."[37] This metaphor expresses the idea that no two situations are exactly the same; circumstances constantly change. Hence, we cannot just apply the moral principles to different situations without examining each particular case. This is not the moment to assess the merits of Heraclitus' philosophy as a whole, but his dictum can illustrate the importance of knowing the "present" sufficiently well in order to act with due prudence.

3. Docility

When we decide on an important matter, it also helps to seek advice, especially if we do not see things with clarity. Do not be too quick to brush aside the suggestions of others. Many people fail because they turn a deaf ear to the truth echoed by a friend, a mentor, a spiritual director, or even a grandparent. It pays to listen, and this implies docility (*docilitas*) to counsel. An integral part of prudence, *docility* literally means "teachability" and hence, *open-mindedness*. A docile person recognizes the complexity of things. He does not presume to know everything, but humbly trusts others who are in a position to help.[38] This attitude stems from the desire to understand the realities well. If a person is closed-minded, it is a way of resisting the truth of things.

Two or three heads are better than one. Even the most brilliant minds cannot see everything. We all need guidance. Every head of state has a team of advisers. Olympic athletes have a coach. Business executives hire consultants. Even the Pope has a spiritual director. Why should we do less when we are trying to settle an important matter? It is best not to rely solely on our own judgment, typical of the know-it-all who flies on the wings of pride.

We do well to seek advice, though not just from anyone. We go to a person with the right qualities, someone who can give us valuable inputs.[39] Aquinas mentions particularly the elderly, who tend to possess more wisdom. In any case, we should be ready to hear what we do not want to hear. Flatterers and yes-men do not help us, only the forthright.[40] The truth may hurt, but it helps us see the wise way to go.

4. Criteria

Prudent men and women possess *criteria* (*ratio*), that is to say, they are able to relate various elements and data and ponder their connection and significance with a critical mind. What is the use of knowing doctrine and having the right information if we cannot use them well?

In our digital world, artificial intelligence (AI) and data analytics can shed light on business trends, give accurate forecasts, or expose root causes by analyzing billions of pieces of data in a matter of seconds. But AI is not about to render the human mind superfluous. It never will! Humans are uniquely creative and ingenious, and we reason out, adapt, infer, empathize, and contextualize in a way that machines and robots cannot. But we must be logical and clear-headed. A reasoning person investigates, compares alternatives, and draws conclusions from premises so as to attain the right goal. This implies basic skills in logical reasoning.

News reports, social media, and conversations may contain logical fallacies, so we need to distinguish what is true from what is false. Perhaps you have heard of some of the more common logical fallacies like *false cause* (*post hoc ergo propter hoc*), *hasty generalization*, and argument *ad hominem*. Just because the car accident occurred when it began to rain does not mean that the mishap was due to rain (*false cause*). *Hasty generalization* is concluding that what is true in one or few instances is true for all. For example:

"My friend smoked all his life and yet he hardly got sick, so smoking is not actually bad." A prudent person avoids the pitfalls of logical fallacies like these and thus forms sound judgments.

5. Shrewdness

Sometimes we need to make a quick decision. A sudden turn of events may require swift action and we do not have the luxury of seeking advice or calm deliberation. Delays can be costly for certain very urgent matters. *Solertia* (sagacity, shrewdness, or mental agility) refers to the ability to form clear-sighted judgments in the face of the unexpected. A doctor is about to perform a coronary surgery when the patient's blood sugar level shoots up. A plane running low on fuel is radioed by the control tower to hover for a while before landing due to runway traffic. Hours before his much-awaited wedding my brother got the tragic news that our dad had just passed away. These are different situations, but they all pose a common challenge: decide fast but wisely.

Pressed to make up his mind quickly, a person may get it right by sheer impulse. That is good luck, not prudence. It is so tempting to just close our eyes and blindly take random action in the face of the unforeseen. It is easy to end up committing acts of injustice, intemperance, or cowardice when pressed to decide on a matter urgently. But prudent individuals are able to think and act well quickly, accustomed as they are to making correct judgments. They are alert, sharp, and swift to decide with clear-sighted vision. We may ascribe to the prudent person the quality of being objective in the face of the unforeseen.[41]

6. Foresight

A key element in any organization is strategic foresight that enables it to build a unique perspective of the future. Strategic planning imagines scenarios and envisions their outcomes, a technique that can serve as a guide in corporate decisions, military operations, stock investments, government policy, or R&D portfolios.[42]

If predicting trends is crucial in organizations, it is more so in moral life. *Foresight*, providence (*providere*), or the ability to see in anticipation is the principal part of the virtue of prudence.[43] Prudence pays attention to upcoming events in order to direct our steps wisely. Of course, we do not see what lies ahead, but we can predict the future events with a forward-looking mind. Through foresight, we assess instinctively whether doing this or that will help attain our goal.

Naturally, there will be incertitude; we are not spared of anxiety. But we do not waver or quit for that reason. In a sense, a prudent approach to life always involves taking some risks. Prudence helps us face the unknown future. Guided by foresight, we launch out and do what needs doing. In this we do not act aimlessly, like someone beating the air, for we count on experience, we weigh things, we seek counsel, we are earnest in our efforts, and most of all, we hope to be aided by divine grace.[44]

7. Circumspection

There can be many ways to accomplish a noble objective. Whether one should approach it this way or that way depends on the circumstances. This implies the ability to judge wisely a given situation. *Circumspection* is the integral part of the virtue of prudence that allows a person to discern what is proper and what is not, considering a host of factors. We call a person *circumspect* if he or she is attentive and careful in choosing the suitable means to achieve a good end.[45]

An act may be prudent in one case, but not quite in another. Buying an online product from the least expensive seller is a wise move, but not if it is offered by a potential website scammer. Generally, it is compassionate to visit a sick friend in the hospital, but it might be ill-advised if he is a Covid patient amidst an upsurge of the deadly pandemic. On the collective level, perhaps there was wisdom in America's isolationism and neutrality at the outbreak of the Second World War, but this policy became untenable after the Japanese bombing of Pearl Harbor on December 7, 1941, and Nazi Germany's declaration of war against the United States just four days later.

Prudence, as we have said, is right reason in action, and the right course of action can vary depending on the current state of affairs. Circumspection is what we need to be able to decide, to pick one avenue instead of another, taking into account all relevant factors. This trait involves surveillance, the capacity to detect subtle clues, distinguish things, and discern the suitable means to an end. "The simple believes everything, but the prudent looks where he is going. A wise man is cautious and turns away from evil, but a fool throws off restraint and is careless" (Prv 14:15–16).

8. Caution[46]

Sometimes our good plans hit a snag or have a downside. Even the most carefully devised schemes encounter hitches and glitches. When you think that you have everything under control, you are probably walking around in the clouds. Life is so complex and full of contingencies in part because the good and the bad coexist. The weeds often grow with the wheat. Just the simple act of taking antihistamine to treat symptoms of allergic rhinitis can trigger drowsiness. Entering your credit card data for an online transaction carries a certain risk.

Thus we need to be careful when making plans, more so if these touch on sensitive moral matters. We do not omit our task or give up on our goals just because we meet hurdles. Rather, we find a way to avoid the danger or at least cushion its negative impact. We proceed but with *caution*, another integral part of the virtue of prudence.

If you need to tell someone tragic news that might cause hysteria, do so delicately and with caution. Strategic bombing of a military target, even with a high-precision weapon, can have civilian casualties as collateral damage, so the operation must be conducted with extreme caution. A terminally ill patient who receives a sedative to alleviate his or her acute pain might die sooner for that reason, so palliative care has to be carried out with great caution.

A prudent person is necessarily cautious. In pursuing a good end, he or she is on the lookout to avoid pitfalls and alert to minimize any harmful effects resulting from his or her good deed.[47] At the same time, we must be cautious with anything that appears good but is in fact evil,[48] a ravening wolf in sheep's clothing (see Mt 7:15). The key is vigilance. Be cautious but not indecisive, wary but purposeful!

In St. Thomas More's *Utopia,* a work of fiction and political satire published in 1516, he gives us a wonderful piece of advice: "You must not abandon the ship in a storm because you cannot control the winds. . . . What you cannot turn to good, you must at least make as little bad as you can."[49]

Acts of Prudence

A wise move, a prudent action, involves three steps: deliberation, judgment, and decision. "Reason is the beginning of every work, and counsel precedes every undertaking" (Sir 37:16).

In anything we do, we go from the most remote and general principles to the most concrete and practical matters. We would be remiss and thoughtless if we made hasty decisions, if we acted without thorough consideration. Of course, despite due diligence we can still commit speculative error. After pondering things, getting someone else's opinion, and so on, our decision may turn out to be faulty or less than the best. Do not worry! Once we do our homework diligently, any misstep is due to sheer human limitation. Imperfect judgment is simply part of an imperfect life in an imperfect world.

That said, before we plunge into something, we had better mull it over, especially if it is important. Never mind perhaps if it is just a question of choosing a dessert. But you do not sign a contract without knowing its terms and conditions. Common sense tells you not to host a stranger just because he seems so nice. It is not wise to rely on a pediatrician to treat your acute respiratory problems. Would you take a broken-down car on a road trip? To act in these cases without due consideration is imprudence.

Faced with an issue to resolve, we may make up our mind swiftly or take our time, but in any case, prudent decisions almost always involve a sequential process of taking counsel carefully, judging wisely, and directing imperatively. Aquinas considers them as aspects of a good intellectual habit.

1. Deliberation (*bene consultare*)

The first step is to inquire, do research, become informed, seek advice, deliberate, recall past cases, foresee likely events, see the connection of various circumstances, and the like. In other words, consider the matter in all its aspects, using the intellectual traits we have considered above as integral parts of the virtue of prudence. The habit of looking for the suitable means to achieve a desired end is called *eubulia*, the first of the three potential parts[50] of the virtue of prudence.[51]

Decision-making requires humility. We do not know everything, nor do we grasp things all at once. We seldom, if ever, understand realities in their true depths. With these in mind, we should not precipitate things, that is, act without careful consideration. Even if we are brilliant, we cannot take shortcuts. It is important to cast about for the best way, the most suitable means to reach an end. "Do nothing without deliberation; and when you have acted, do not regret it" (Sir 32:19).

Right-minded people know how to act in normal circumstances without much ado. They can decide quickly since their options are narrowed down to a few alternatives, leaving out obviously bad choices. There is nothing to discuss when it comes to evil things; we immediately shut the doors that lead to this precipice.[52] Not so in the case of the worldly and unprincipled. They tend to entertain options that may look appealing but are bad or even deplorable.[53]

Let us say that a professor cancels his or her lecture at the last minute due to an emergency, leaving his or her students suddenly free. While some students might opt to study or engage in other worthwhile pursuits, others might waste their time or worse, do stupid things. Their lax attitude leads to many poor alternatives.

Prudence implies rectitude of intention and purity of heart. The better a person's character, the less he or she considers bad moral options, for they will be the first to be excluded.

2. Judgment (*recte iudicare*)

The second step in prudence is to decide or judge. *Judgment* follows deliberation and is the act of choosing the appropriate conduct based on the data gathered and evidence weighed. "Given the situation, how should I behave?" "After thinking things over, what must I do?" We cannot deliberate indefinitely; at some point we need to pick a course of action. "Failure to make a judgment is called indecision. Procrastination, perfectionism, and fear of failure are common indecision traps."[54] Most of us have met people who are inclined to sit on the fence and cannot make up their mind.

Most of our decisions deal with ordinary things. Prudence in making judgments about simple matters is called *synesis*, the second potential part of the virtue of prudence.[55] It is the right mind regarding what to do in cases governed by common law or by a lower power of judgment. A person with this quality is called *sensible*. People who lack this virtue are "senseless." We refer to *synesis* when we say, "Taking a work leave is the most sensible thing to do when you feel unwell," or negatively, "It is senseless to order six dishes on large platters when only two are eating." Making good decisions about ordinary things is called common sense.

Occasionally though, we face situations that are exceptional and warrant setting aside a particular rule[56] in favor of a more specialized approach. A higher power of judgment called *gnome* is needed for those matters that require higher moral principles, above the common laws.[57] Gnome implies a keen sense of judgment and is the third potential part of the virtue of prudence.[58]

For example, a company may require Covid vaccination for all its employees to ensure a healthy work environment. But if this policy leads to mass resignations and cripples the company's operation due to lack of personnel, it may decide to relax this guideline. This delicate decision is gnome. Or, if an athlete training for the Olympics is injured three weeks before the sporting event, he or she and his or her team (coach, sports therapist, and so forth) will have to decide whether it is prudent to compete or find a substitute. As a rule, the person hurt should fully recover. Deciding on extraordinary cases like this requires a keen judgment called gnome.

One historical and dramatic example of gnome was the way Pius XII dealt with the Nazis during the Second World War. He used diplomacy to aid the war victims, deplored racial murders, helped the Jews secretly, and saved thousands of lives. If he seemed to remain neutral and did not explicitly name the Nazis, it was a calculated move to avoid fierce reprisals and avert further killings. Such a complicated moral situation has no easy, one-size-fits-all solution. It requires a higher ability of reason to judge events. Wise decisions that constitute an exception to the rule involve precisely gnome. Gnome helps us avoid becoming too rigid in applying moral norms to delicate circumstances; it allows for flexibility in a prudent way.

3. Command (*imperare, praecipere*)

The third step in the exercise of prudence is to command. Deciding what to do is one thing, deciding to act is another. Once we have figured out a problem, we must move promptly. It is pointless to linger unnecessarily. Action, we say, speaks more than words. What makes a person morally exemplary is not ultimately his or her good desires and good judgment, but his or her good deeds.

As an act of the virtue of prudence, *command* carries out what has been determined to be the most convenient approach. It is a sort of court order that implements the final verdict of a judicial proceeding, to borrow legal jargon. Prudence is a process that starts with a cognitive aspect and ends with an imperative character.

Some people are trapped in a cycle of decision and indecision. Hesitation paralyzes them. At times we may have to change our mind, especially if new data surface or circumstances change. But this has nothing to do with fickle-mindedness. Until we carry out our good plans, it cannot really be said that we act prudently. The command of the will to execute and set things in motion is the most important element of prudence, since this virtue is a habit of the practical (not theoretical) intellect.

Sometimes the fear of making a mistake holds us back. We put things off and make other people wait. But inaction can be worse than an imperfect decision. It can spoil a whole project and chip away at our credibility. It sounds funny, but have you experienced dining with your friends in a restaurant and no one knows what to order? The clock is ticking, you are all hungry, and the waiter is kept on hold. Indecision can delay simple things like this. But, of course, it also affects more serious things in life, as when we decide which career to pursue, where to live, what business to invest in, or which medical treatment to follow.

Certainly prudence is not a gateway to avoid commitments, lest things go awry. Individuals who refuse to take responsibilities spend their life in "safe zones," away from important tasks. They are weak, negligent, and cowardly. Culpable omission and willful neglect are forms of imprudence.[59]

Forms of Imprudence

Broadly speaking, vices against the virtue of prudence can be either by defect or by excess. There are many forms of imprudence, as we shall now discuss.

1. Faulty Prudence (Vices by Defect)[60]

When we make a decision in a way that is defective in terms of *deliberation*, *judgment*, or *action*, we sin against prudence. As we have said, a prudent act presupposes a sequential process of *counsel*, *judgment*, and *command*, all of which are necessary elements of a prudent act. When any such element is lacking, we have a case called *faulty prudence*, and it comes by way of precipitation, thoughtlessness, negligence, and inconstancy.

A person who decides hastily, without thinking things over, becoming well informed, assessing the situation, and foreseeing the turn of events, falls into *rashness* or *precipitation*, the first vice against the virtue of prudence by defect. Otherwise known as *impetuosity*, this vice is typical of those who jump into action a bit too quickly, without considering adequately the available means.[61] Lacking in deliberation, they tend to act driven by sheer whim. In a sense, an impetuous person is a slave of his or her passion. As the old saying goes, "Fools rush in where angels fear to tread."

Someone drives to a superstore with a big holiday sale. He or she grabs items that look like bargains, only to realize back home that most of the purchases were unneeded. Impulse buying is a classic example of rashness and precipitation.

Maybe we have thought things over but still made a poor decision. Imprudence may also be rooted not in our lack of deliberation but in an error of judgment, either *synesis* (ordinary cases) or *gnome* (extraordinary cases). We may size up the problem but not well enough—we lack circumspection and caution[62]—such that the solution we choose is wrong. This case is called *thoughtlessness*, the second vice against the virtue of prudence by defect. Thoughtlessness differs from rashness in that the former is ill-thought-of (it goes against *right judgment*) while the latter is ill-advised (it goes against *counsel*).

On October 1, 2015, the US-flagged container ship *El Faro* sank while sailing into the eyewall of category 3 Hurricane Joaquin east of the Bahamas, killing all thirty-three crew members. An investigation later showed that the ship's company and the vessel's captain had been forewarned of the brewing storm. A big cargo ship can usually handle rough waves, but here the captain's decision to sail right into the hurricane was a *thoughtless*, fatal call.

What if a person has pored over a question and has decided what to do, but then falls short of commanding the action? This case is called *negligence*, the third vice against the virtue of prudence by defect. *Deliberation* and *judgment* do not necessarily lead to action. In fact, we can over-deliberate on an issue but do nothing about it in the end for lack of drive. Contrary to command, negligence is the failure of the intellect to direct the will to execute a right judgment, to perform an act when it is prudent to do so. We have cited a few examples above (see "Command [*imperare, praecipere*]"), but in day-to-day life we find examples aplenty. Sometimes we start the day with a list of things to do, yet by bedtime we are unable to cross out any item on the list for no other reason than negligence.

Inconstancy is the fourth vice against the virtue of prudence by defect. You might think this is synonymous with negligence. The two concepts are indeed very similar, but there is a fine distinction. Negligence is failing to command; *inconstancy* is failing to carry out what is commanded. The vice of inconstancy goes directly against command, which as we have stated, is the principal aspect of prudence, since this virtue is a habit of the practical (not theoretical) intellect. A moral action is rendered incomplete by our refusal to fulfill the command of reason owing to love of comfort or attachment to pleasure. We are inconstant if we fail to apply the dictates of prudence and we abandon quite easily, for vain reasons, our good resolutions. This is often the culprit behind our inability to carry out what we know we should.

2. Plain Imprudence (Vices by Excess)[63]

A scriptural passage (Rom 8:5–8) speaks of true and false prudence. The latter refers to *prudence of the flesh*, which is a vice against the virtue of prudence by excess and consists in the ability to find suitable means for twisted ends. *False prudence* is a clever way to satisfy our disordered passions. It is deceitful, manipulative, and selfish. Take note that right judgment as regards the means does not always imply moral integrity.

A person can be very "careful" and "prudent" in destroying proofs of marital infidelity, like text messages or receipts. Bank robbers can "wisely" steal money through "discreet" note-passing to the teller, rather than brazenly holding up everyone with assault weapons.

Also called *carnal prudence*, this vice means that a person sets his heart on worthless things, takes advantage of others, and makes earthly goods his or her chief reason for existence. It is a grave error that nips the virtue of prudence in the bud. Aquinas observes that false prudence is found only in sinners, for it "consists in effective reasoning with respect to the means to attain evil ends."[64] People who are "diligent" and "crafty" for the wrong reason are not prudent in the true sense of the word, but prudent only as "sons of this world" or "sons of this generation" (Lk 16:8).

If *prudence of the flesh* is cleverness in seeking an evil purpose, *cunning* (*astutia*) is cleverness in seeking any goal, be it good or evil.[65] Cunning is yet another vice against the virtue of prudence by excess. We all know the principle that "the end does not justify the means." We cannot resort to insidious tactics and cagey methods to achieve our goals, no matter how "lofty." Prudence requires that both the end and the means of human acts conform to the truth of things. But an astute person is wily and devious in his or her ways.

Cunning in the form of words is called *deceit*; when employed in deeds, it becomes *fraud*. The two are so intertwined that deception is often used to gain advantage to the detriment of someone else. In business and finance, false insurance claims, tax fraud, or identity theft leading to unauthorized purchases are types of fraud that involve deceit. In canon law, to further illustrate this point, marrying an American citizen without real love and conjugal commitment, but just as a furtive way to obtain United States citizenship, is *simulation*.[66] Here the groom or the bride feigns marital consent or a wedding vow for ulterior motives, a legal ground for marriage nullity.

False prudence and cunning are rooted in greed and inordinate self-love. Unbridled desire for wealth, fame, power, success, physique, beauty, or position often drives people to resort to unconscionable means. When a person is excessively ambitious, he or she is anxious and restless, his or her mind tends to be obscured, the will twisted, and behavior depraved. He or she overvalues earthly things and secures his or her own future, trusting little in God's providence. The key word is "excessive." It is not wrong to have possessions, seek prestige, and look pretty or handsome; what is unhealthy is overdoing them or seeking them in a disordered way. We do well to strive to earn more, but not as if money were all that mattered in life. Remember that the virtue of prudence avoids extremes[67] by pointing us to the mean of reason.

Subjective Parts[68]

The subjective parts of prudence are the various species or kinds of prudence that apply to specific human actions. Up until now we have mostly discussed *personal prudence*, the virtue that each individual needs in order to make correct decisions and live a morally good life. Yet "[n]one of us lives to himself, and none of us dies to himself" (Rom 14:7). We are surrounded by our family, friends, colleagues, acquaintances, and the like. We may be part of a civic group, a country club, a corporate organization, or a professional guild. And certainly we are citizens of a country. There are decisions and actions that have social impact and affect the common good. Hence, in additional to *personal* or *individual prudence*, there is also *social* or *collective prudence*.[69] Leaders and those in positions of authority especially need to observe prudence and make wise decisions. Their judgments and behavior can do a lot of good or a lot of harm to people under their influence.

Social prudence, in turn, exhibits several types. Firstly, there is *governmental prudence*, which is proper to those in civil authority. Legislation should take into account the requirements of the common good. Raising business taxes might increase government revenue, but it can also harm consumers if the economic measure triggers inflation. Given the complexities of any political order, leaders must serve society with a far-reaching vision, professional competence, and moral integrity.

However, government prudence needs to be reciprocated by ordinary citizens who share in the duty to promote the commonwealth. Our leaders will be hard put to succeed in their task of governance if we do not prudently cooperate and fulfill our civic duties. This second type of social prudence is called *political prudence*.

Thirdly, there is *domestic prudence*, which is required of those who lead smaller societies or intermediate institutions like a family. Running a household requires wise decisions on spending, work, education, medical care, holiday trips, and the like.

Finally, we can speak of special types of prudence that are specific to particular fields of endeavor, such as law, medicine, trade, military, teaching, and so forth.[70] Handling a lawsuit requires prudence. So also prescribing medicine, making an investment, conducting an army operation, directing a graduate thesis, and so forth. The common thread of all these decisions is that they affect not just ourselves but other people as well, and so they carry a significant weight for good or bad.

The Moral Good

If prudence is doing the right thing in the right way at the right moment, what is the right thing in the first place? If a prudent decision is basically choosing a moral good here and now, how do we know what is good? This question is primordial, for the whole edifice of moral life, and hence the virtue of prudence, relies on our knowledge of what constitutes the good.

Is a homosexual act good or bad? Can a pregnant woman abort her baby at will? Why is drunk driving prohibited? Should news outlets give accurate reports? Who says that premarital sex is wrong? Is it OK to use pirated software? Am I accountable if I take office supplies? How do we determine the moral good?

Quite interestingly, the virtue of prudence does not give us the answer; it is not the business of prudence to show us the ultimate goal of human life.[71] Prudence presupposes it. The role of this cardinal virtue is to point out the fitting means to reach our final end.[72] In the same way that the GPS tells us the best route to reach a destination—and does not select our destination—so also the virtue of prudence indicates how best to achieve our final end; it does not determine it.

Therefore, we can be prudent only if we love and desire the moral good previously and concomitantly. We would only apply right reason to action if we had upright intention in the first place.[73] The *intentio finis* is a precondition of the virtue of prudence.[74] Before prudence can operate in a concrete situation, a person must want to be just, brave, honest, temperate, loyal, and the like. A person would switch the TV channel to avoid smutty shows only if he or she wanted to be chaste. If you realize as you step out of a store that the cashier gave you too much change, you would return the excess only if you are fair minded. Indeed, right appetite is part and parcel of prudence.[75]

Yet the question remains: How do we know what is good? We do not spend our whole life trying to figure out the ultimate good, in what true human fulfillment consists. That is taken care of. Knowledge of humanity's basic desires, which point to our fundamental goals, cannot be the result of an ability still to be acquired and developed as we grow up.[76] Our finite mind is compelled to know the truth of our being. We are not at liberty to ignore the truth to which we are naturally inclined. This drive is beyond the power of reason to oppose.[77]

To help us understand how the moral good is grasped, we can use the schema of the Belgian theologian Servais Pinckaers (1925–2008), which explains how humanity's natural inclinations correspond to moral precepts, basic human rights, and human virtues.[78] It all starts with the fact that we humans are inclined to goodness and happiness (only a fool would take this proposition to task). This inclination is manifested in certain basic tendencies that we all share. Next, we love and desire what we are naturally inclined to do. Then, these things must be good for us, we need them, and they help us grow as persons. Finally, these inclinations ought to be fostered, these goods must be sought, and such needs must be respected.

In Aristotle's theory of virtues, every person as he or she happens to be is distinct from the person as he or she should be.[79] Morality is *teleological* (Greek *telos*: end, purpose, goal). Humanity's goodness has reference to our full human potential, inherent purpose, or *raison d'être*. The ultimate basis of upright conduct is not what we feel like doing but who we are meant to be; not what we think is right but what is right.

Our inclination to goodness and happiness, which contain all other tendencies, is expressed in the foremost principle of morality that no person can ignore: "Do good and avoid evil!" We all know this first principle of natural law, a knowledge called synderesis, which we discussed earlier. From this self-evident, overriding first principle are derived the primary moral precepts that we shall now explain.

A person's natural tendencies are objects of human desire and are essential for our fulfillment. Referred to as intelligible goods, they are perceived not by the senses (sight, sound, smell, etcetera) but by the intellect. Consequently, they are desired not by the sense appetite but by the rational appetite, the will. Thus, we hold and taste bread and butter, but we value and esteem love and friendship. Since the intelligible goods are intrinsic to us (as in, aspects of the Person), they are called human goods, and since they are naturally desired, we naturally know them.

It is pretty obvious that everyone (of sound mind) wants to live as long as possible. We are willing to give up practically everything just to stay alive. Never mind spending a huge amount to pay the hospital bills if that is the only way to recover our health. We also eat, drink, and sleep in response to our deepest inclination to life. That is basic instinct and is in keeping with human dignity.

Likewise, we want to know the truth (we hate being lied to) and to get a good education (earn a degree, Google search), to have friends and associate with other people (join a club, attend a party), to settle down and form a family (court a girl, get engaged), to see beautiful things and enjoy pastimes (visit a museum, play basketball), to be in control of ourselves and attain inner harmony (seek therapy, go to confession), and finally to transcend ourselves and seek the Supreme Good who is God (pray, go to church). Therefore, the human goods include human life, knowledge of truth, sociability, contemplation of beauty, leisure (play and art), marriage, personal integrity, and religion.

Deeply embedded in our nature, these inclinations are starting points, basic motivations, and primary principles of practical reason underlying authentic human acts.[80] Ethics is built on these human goods. Morally upright acts are those that respect and protect such natural moral goods, just as evil deeds stem from the failure to seek (if not the drive to violate) these goods.

Corollary to the primary principles are secondary precepts that are knowable by all men. In all cultures and civilizations across history, for example, justice (respecting the goods of others, be it physical or spiritual) is highly valued. Human beings always demand fair treatment. This includes the right to property and the right to the truth, corresponding respectively to the seventh and eight commandments of the Decalogue. For this reason, stealing and lying are evil deeds. Everyone knows that, unless he or she is crazy.

We know by reason that God exists as the Supreme Good, so our relationship with God is with the greatest human good, and he ought to be loved above all things. This corresponds to the first three commandments. Religious freedom ought to be safeguarded. So, when state governments closed the churches but allowed beauty salons and nail spas to remain open during the pandemic, people cried foul and demanded freedom of worship.

Human life is an intelligible good and should thus be protected from all harms and threats. Here we have the fifth commandment. So, murder, abortion, euthanasia, and any physical violence are starkly evil. If men and women naturally desire marriage as a true human good, then the marital bond and sexuality must be reverenced. For this reason, the sixth and ninth commandments prohibit adultery and lustful desires respectively. Any form of sexual abuse is an offense.

The Ten Commandments are not suggestions but orders that bind us to obedience. Besides, the Decalogue could have been known by reason even if Moses had not received it from God on Mount Sinai. It is reasonable and proper to human dignity to do what we naturally know to be the right thing to do.[81]

When the United Nations General Assembly adopted the Universal Declaration of Human Rights (UDHR) on December 10, 1948, it enshrined in that landmark document fundamental truths about human beings. Reeling from the horrors and ravages of the Second World War, the community of nations gathered around the table to lay down in clear and unambiguous terms basic human rights and freedoms. Specifically, the UN sought to protect the right to life, family, and property, to freedom of thought, speech, worship, movement, conscience, association, and an adequate standard of living.

Rooted in the dignity of the Person, these human rights and liberties are inherent and inalienable. Neither society nor the state confer these rights; they simply recognize what the Person already possesses by nature. That the UN document squares with the primary and secondary moral principles highlights the fact that these are *knowable* (accessible to reason), *universal* (apply to all people), *immutable* (unchanging), and *obligatory* (binding and imperative). Ultimately, the UN Charter is a recognition of the natural law, the truth about humanity, and objective morality.

Sadly, the UN principles have not always been followed and human rights violations are widespread. Hence, Benedict XVI reminded the world body of its avowed mission, saying that when rights are presented merely in legal terms, they become weak propositions devoid of ethical and rational foundations. Human rights are sacrificed for utilitarian motives and cease to be an expression of justice.[82]

Moral Relativism

The foregoing analysis of the moral good is important since the virtue of prudence seeks the most suitable means to achieve the good end *hic et nunc*—here and now.

Unfortunately, not everyone accepts the idea that there exist moral absolutes accessible to all and valid for all cultures. There is a crisis of *moral relativism*, the theory that holds that morality is subjective, depending on one's cultural values, historical milieu, and individual choices. People may licitly disagree on anything. Nobody is right or wrong objectively. There is no single truth that binds everyone. Ethical pluralism and tolerance are the order of the day. Or so claim the moral relativists.

Moral relativism is among the major issues in moral theology that acquired prominence in the years following the
Second Vatican Council (1962–1965). Questions were raised
as regards man's capacity to discern the good, the existence of
evil, human freedom, conscience, mortal sin, and the Church's
moral authority.

In response to the confusion, St. John Paul II came out with
the milestone encyclical *Veritatis Splendor* (1993), defending the
idea that there are indeed absolute moral truths knowable by all.
The moral law is universal and immutable. No matter how alien-
ated a person is from God, "[i]n the depths of his heart there
always remains a yearning for the absolute truth and a thirst to
attain full knowledge of it."[83] In the same vein, certain human
acts are intrinsically evil regardless of our intentions and circumstances. Moreover, John Paul II minced no words to reaffirm the
authority of the magisterium of the Catholic Church to make
definitive pronouncements on moral issues.

Moral relativism gives rise to false goods or apparent goods
(as opposed to real human goods), that is to say, objects of
human desire that seem to benefit and perfect man, but actually
destroy the human person. Adulterous affairs, friendship with
the mafia, substance abuse, and pornography may look appealing, but they are ruinous. Only what is truly perfective of the
human person is considered a true good, like honest friendship,
clean entertainment, fidelity, self-control, and moderation.

When we reject the natrual law, we lose our moral bearing
and the sense of sin. We then fall into the quicksand of hedonism
(pleasure is the highest good) and legal positivism (anything
legal is good). As a consequence, people give free rein to their
whims and caprice, finding justification for all sorts of moral
aberration. The natural law, which is written in our hearts (see
Rom 2:15), becomes an obstacle to freedom, wrongly understood as the ability to do whatever a person wants.

Once the objective truth is trampled upon, the floodgate is left open to abortion, divorce, euthanasia, same-sex marriage, and the like. Moral relativism is a regime of strange paradoxes. In it human fetuses are aborted, yet test tube babies are produced. Life expectancy is increased, but the terminally ill and elderly are "mercifully" killed. Marriage is broken apart by divorce, yet same-sex unions are celebrated. One absurd example is Germany's requirement for a person to be fully vaccinated for Covid to qualify for assisted suicide; one has to be healthy if he or she wants to die. From whichever side you see it, the world is in disarray because humanity clings to false goods in a classic form of moral relativism. The crises of contemporary societies are rooted in a flawed anthropology, humanity's failure to grasp our true identity.

But the crisis of truth is ultimately traced to individuals. The "structures of evil" in the world are offshoots of personal sins of billions of men and women that make up society. Institutions and technologies do not make rational choices; only people do. Whether it is Congress, tech giants, Wall Street, media networks, or Hollywood, policies are being crafted by persons who make good or bad choices, prudent or imprudent decisions.

Role of Conscience

We have seen in our previous discussions that prudence inclines us to think and act well in every situation that requires a moral stance. As right reason in action, the virtue of prudence tells us what to do, when to do it, and how to do it. Now we might ask, "How does *prudence* differ from *conscience*? Aren't the two concepts basically the same?"

Prudence and *conscience* are intimately linked, but they are two distinct notions. Prudence is a virtue, a power, a stable habit of the practical intellect that guides us to decide how best to act in a given instance. Whereas, conscience is a judgment or ruling of the practical intellect on the lawfulness of a concrete act. It is possible for us to have a correct, well-formed conscience and yet to be imprudent at the same time, if we do not act on our good judgment. But it is impossible to be prudent and not have a correct conscience.[84] We can say that prudence includes the judgment of conscience as one of its proper acts and puts this judgment in practice in the most fitting way.

Conscience is every person's most secret core and inner sanctuary in which he or she hears God's voice. It is our deepest interior where no one has access, except myself and the Lord. The right to act in conscience and in freedom is necessary for us to make moral decisions. Hence, it is a basic and inviolable human right. This is what inspires advocates of conscientious objection, like young men who oppose military conscription for unjust wars, nurses who refuse to participate in abortion, or writers who decline to be party to slanderous or defamatory articles.

More specifically, "Conscience is a judgment of reason whereby the human person recognizes the moral quality of a concrete act that he is going to perform, is in the process of performing, or has already completed."[85] As a witness to the truth, conscience warns and admonishes, reproves and condemns.

We can get a glimpse of the *reflective* role of conscience (it looks at the past) from the Book of Genesis, when God accosted our primogenitors. *"Where are you?"* (Gn 3:9, my emphasis). *"What is this that you have done?"* (Gn 3:13, my emphasis), the Lord God asked Adam and Eve respectively in the wake of their transgressions. And from Cain, God demanded an answer: *"Where is Abel your brother?"* (Gn 4:9, my emphasis). But conscience also has a *prospective* role: it anticipates our plans. Long before Judas betrayed Jesus, Our Lord knew the sinister designs of his disciple: "Did I not choose you, the twelve, and one of you is a devil?" (Jn 6:70). Christ hinted to Judas that nothing escapes

God's eyes. Jesus exposed the traitor's dark schemes, if only to save him: "He who has dipped his hand in the dish with me, will betray me" (Mt 26:23; Mk 14:20).

Ethical choices put us in a bind: we need to make a decision, and it will either conform to right reason or deviate from it, either follow the divine law or disobey it. We can do what we want, but we cannot call good what is bad or call bad what is good.[86] Our choices are right or wrong in so far as they conform to the moral truth laid bare to us by our conscience. You can drive through a red traffic light, but you are not at liberty to change the red to green.

Therefore, our conscience does not make its own subjective rules of right and wrong; rather, it judges our conduct based on the objective moral law. While some people take conscience as God's invitation to embrace his will, others consider it as a license to unbridled freedom, to do what they "wish" or "feel right." In his Letter to the Duke of Norfolk, St. John Henry Newman wrote that "[conscience] is a messenger from Him, Who, both in nature and in grace, speaks to us behind a veil, and teaches and rules us by His representatives. Conscience is the aboriginal Vicar of Christ."[87] If we receive a message, we read it or listen to it; we do not modify it to suit our tastes.

The *Catechism of the Catholic Church* states, "In all he says and does, man is obliged to follow faithfully what he knows to be just and right."[88] If what we think to be right turns out to be indeed right, our conscience is *correct*, meaning that its judgment conforms to right reason or the moral good (true judgment). But if we consider as right what is in fact wrong—that is, if our judgment does not coincide with the objective moral truth—our conscience is *erroneous* (false judgement). Though our innate ability to apprehend the first principles of morality (do good and avoid evil) is not subject to error, our judgment in particular cases can be flawed. In fact, the human conscience can be twisted and deformed due to ignorance and bad habits.

Confronted with moral choices, we can also be either *certain* or *doubtful* as to what is right and wrong. Our conscience is *certain* if we sincerely believe that something is right ("I'm sure I'm correct") and there is no fear of being mistaken. On the other hand, the conscience is *doubtful* if we are clueless which way to go, which side to take ("I have doubts"; "I don't know what's the right thing to do"), or if our intellect cannot see clearly whether a given action is good or bad and so it withholds making a judgment.

When we act, the basic rule is to obey the judgment of our conscience if it is certain (not doubtful). If the intellect concludes with certitude[89] that something must be done or avoided, then the person must so behave.[90] If, deep in your heart, you sincerely believe it right, then do it! You would sin if you act against the dictate of your conscience, since it is the proximate norm of morality and has an imperative character. This principle holds true even if a person who is subjectively certain turns out to be objectively erroneous.[91] In sports like soccer or basketball, the referee or umpire can make a bad call, but just the same, their decision stands. Similarly, if our conscience enjoins us to act this or that way, we have to abide by its judgment, even if in the end that judgment turns out to be mistaken.

Following the line of argument above, if a person believes that it is OK to use artificial contraception, not knowing that it is an intrinsically evil act, is he or she blameworthy? If a Catholic omits going to Mass on the feast of the Immaculate Conception, unaware that it is a day of obligation, is he or she guilty? If a motorist turns right on a red light in New York City, convinced that is it is allowed, and the police pull him over, will it help to say that he or she was not aware of the ban?

The answer depends on whether these people should have known better. If they are ignorant of the law due to lack of diligence to know what is true, good, and lawful, we have a case of *vincible ignorance*. Such defect is inexcusable, so they are culpable of their offenses.[92] Had they taken the trouble to find out the truth, the person, the Catholic, and the motorist would have figured out the right thing to do.

Ignorance of sound doctrine and the moral teachings of the Church is at the root of many errors in moral life. Over a century ago, St. Pius X said that "the will cannot be upright nor the conduct good when the mind is shrouded in the darkness of crass ignorance,"[93] adding that it is vain to expect someone to fulfill his duties if he does not even know them. Closer to our time, Mary Ann Glendon, professor emeritus at Harvard Law School and former United States ambassador to the Holy See, asked a rhetorical question: How can Catholics defend their beliefs if even the most highly educated men and women among them have but a primitive, kindergarten-level apprehension of their own faith?[94]

On the other hand, if a person commits an error due to *invincible ignorance*, he or she is not culpable. This happens when the individual is not aware of the law through no fault of his or her own. If it is impossible or very hard for us to discover the norm despite our assiduous effort,[95] we are not liable for any misdeed born of our ignorance. Any evil action we commit in a state of invincible ignorance constitutes a material sin, but not a formal sin, since there is no willful violation of the moral law.[96] Still, the disorder must be remedied; we need to conquer our ignorance and form our conscience.

Formation of Conscience

Our proclivity to error only highlights the need to deepen our knowledge of moral and doctrinal truths. In a society characterized by moral relativism and where secularism is the "new religion," forming our conscience becomes all the more pressing a task. We need a critical mind so that we do not just take in whatever is dished out by the mass media, public opinion, or lawmakers. We ought to separate the wheat from the chaff, to discern what is true from what is false.

External influences are often abetted by the complicity of our personal weaknesses. Faced with moral demands, it is tempting for us to follow our own judgment and ignore authoritative teachings.[97] Many people also equate "freedom of conscience" with the false notion of a self-sufficient mind not anchored on the moral truth.

But human dignity requires rectitude of the moral conscience, a conscience that is based on the truth. As stated earlier, the moral conscience does not create a personal law, but rather applies God's law inscribed in our hearts (Rom 2:14–16), that is to say, it bears witness to the authority of the natural law.[98] Sometimes we try to convince ourselves that what we do is right, brushing aside the differing voice of our conscience. This is self-deception. Prudence requires humility, openness to the truth, and the courage to accept it.

Formation of conscience is everybody's duty and is a lifelong task. It is especially needed by people whose conscience tends to issue a defective or biased judgment. This occurs when a person feels guilty of a sin he or she did not really commit (*scrupulous conscience*) or thinks he or she did nothing wrong despite his or her blatant offense (*lax conscience*).

Our ability to form correct judgments is developed to the extent that we have a good grasp of the moral law. One sure tool to acquire sound doctrine is the *Catechism of the Catholic Church*, which is offered to all the faithful who wish to deepen their knowledge of the unfathomable riches of salvation (see Eph 3:8). The light of faith liberates humanity from the darkness of ignorance and the slavery of sin.[99]

We need to ask God to enlighten our minds, firm up our will, and tame our passions. Moral rectitude includes the effort to remove obstacles to right judgment such as sinful habits, worldly desires, unhealthy attachments, doubts of faith, and resistance to the truth. "Make me to know thy ways, O Lord; teach me thy paths" (Ps 25:4). We can only resist the seductions of the flesh, the world, and the devil if we strive to practice the virtues and cultivate a deep spiritual life.

A time-tested means of formation such as spiritual direction is equally important in acquiring a delicate conscience. The role of the spiritual director is to accompany us on our life's journey, helping us to navigate through the sea of confusion and reach our final destination. Recall our discussion on counsel as an integral part of the virtue of prudence. Having a good spiritual director is a measure of prudence for someone who wants to live an upright moral life and seek personal holiness. The spiritual director, they say, is there to comfort the disturbed and to disturb the comfortable (the lax and lukewarm).

Even more important, for Catholics at least, is the frequent recourse to the sacrament of confession, for it washes our soul clean from all dirt and filth, helping us grow humanly and spiritually. This presupposes a contrite heart and the effective desire to amend our ways. Regular confession has untold benefits:

> [G]enuine self-knowledge is increased, Christian humility grows, bad habits are corrected, spiritual neglect and tepidity are resisted, the conscience is purified, the will is strengthened, a salutary self-control is attained, and grace is increased in virtue of the Sacrament itself.[100]

Naturally, it is helpful to examine our conscience often to ensure a fruitful confession. We ought to uncover the roots of our behavior. Why do I fall into it again and again? What are my deepest dispositions? Am I truly sorry for my sins? In examining our conscience we ask ourselves:

> Where is my heart? We thus discover its inclination and penetrate to its central core, from which arise our words and actions. It shows us what is essential in our pursuit of perfection; it keeps us continually contrite; it makes us grateful when we realize that we are faithful; and it leads us to pray for grace and strength.[101]

In this regard, we do well to ask for the gifts of the Holy Spirit such as wisdom, understanding, counsel, and knowledge.

Our character and personality are also shaped by the level of culture and breadth of knowledge we acquire. While most do not need the erudition of a specialist, it is helpful to have a list of spiritual and cultural books to be read according to a plan. In our day prudence requires a well-formed intellect, mind, heart, and conscience.

Christian Prudence

So far, we have considered the virtue of prudence mostly on the natural plane. It is acquired through experience by the repetition of good acts. A person who often makes the right choices becomes wise via the habit of good decision-making. This is possible due to the capacity of human reason to discern what is truly good and pursue it. *Natural prudence* has as its end human perfection.

But the virtue has a higher form called *infused prudence* or *Christian prudence* that operates on the supernatural plane. We do not acquire it through effort but receive it as God's gift. Supernatural prudence acts with the light of faith and is united to charity, so only people in the state of grace possess it. The end of the infused virtue of prudence is not just human plenitude, but whatever leads to eternal salvation. Simply stated, it helps us to become not just a good person but a saint.

In reality, the natural and the supernatural virtues of prudence blend together as a living reality in a baptized Christian in the state of grace. Prudence grows over time as the person wisely tackles multiple problems, increases in sanctifying grace, and acquires a deeper interior life. Moreover, a *gift of counsel* grows in proportion to the theological virtue of charity. One of the seven gifts of the Holy Spirit, the gift of counsel (*donum consilii*) is like divine advice that aids man's rational judgment on how to act best in every instance. This supernatural counsel helps and perfects natural prudence.

The distinction between natural and infused prudence has practical implications. What may appear as imprudent to the pagan and secular world may be prudent from the Christian standpoint, and vice versa. It is no wonder that saints often do things that are madness in the eyes of other men, even good men. Or that the saints despise what the rest of mortals tend to idolize. To cite one example, in his encyclical *Humane Vitae* (1968) Pope St. Pius VI declared the use of artificial birth control methods to be gravely immoral, reaffirming the Church's traditional moral teaching on the sanctity of life and the procreative and unitive nature of conjugal love. His decision was fiercely criticized in the West and gave rise to open dissent, even within the Church. Paul VI may have been a lone voice in some ways, but he was and is on the side of the truth. He may have been intransigent toward sin, but he was merciful and compassionate toward sinners. "For the wisdom of this world is folly with God" (1 Cor 3:19).

The world is teeming with intellectuals, scholars, and thinkers who are atheists; they are a classic example of the "wise" by worldly standards who are inept at judging things and events from a deeper spiritual perspective. Higher IQ does not automatically translate into wise decisions. Conversely, a person may have scant human and doctrinal knowledge and yet be full of wisdom. C. S. Lewis graphically put it like this: "God will not love you any the less, or have less use for you, if you happen to have been born with a very second-rate brain."[102] In the same vein, children in the state of grace have practical wisdom. They may be inexperienced, but they can do what truly matters: shun evil, choose holy things, and seek God in simple ways.[103]

Christian prudence involves a childlike trust in God, leading us along a path that we would not choose for ourselves. We take actions that we might not consider without infused prudence and the gift of counsel.[104] For God's logic is not man's logic. In any case, like sheep in the midst of wolves, we need to be shrewd as serpents, yet innocent as doves (Mt 10:16).

CHAPTER 2

The Virtue of Justice

Everybody knows the Golden Rule: *Do unto others what you would have others do unto you.* This maxim is called an ethic of reciprocity and it appears in major religions, cultures, and traditions across the world. One of the basic values we learned as a child is to be fair with everyone (share your candies, return the toy, don't hurt others) Sometimes the Golden Rule is inverted to express a negative injunction, also called the Silver Rule: *Do not treat others the way you would not have them treat you.* Jesus laid down this universal principle in the Sermon on the Mount (Mt 7:12; Lk 6:31).

The Golden Rule, in a way, introduces the *cardinal virtue of justice*, for the fundamental precept evokes the idea of being just, fair, honest, upright, equitable, conscientious, and impartial. In the broad sense of the word, justice is the principle that people should receive what they deserve, in the same way that we can claim what belongs to us. Aquinas tackles this important topic in sixty-six questions of his *Summa Theologica*, helping us to establish a peaceful and equitable social order.

The human being is social by nature. We do not live in isolation but need others to attain our full human potential. Some people are outgoing and extroverted, while others tend to be reserved and withdrawn. But regardless of one's personality traits, sociability is a requirement of a person's dignity. St. Augustine wrote that God derived the whole human race from one individual, so that they might be united not only by similarity of nature but also by ties of relationship.[1] Hence, everybody interacts with everyone else as part of a collective body, creating a network of interpersonal relations that must be governed by justice to ensure social peace and harmony. Justice is a complex virtue, but it flows like a spring from a font when people see things from the perspective of their fellow humans and act in consequence.

When we hear the word *justice*, often what comes to mind are social issues like hunger and poverty, racial inequality, unemployment, or public corruption. Often, news reports carry stories of armed conflict, illegal immigration, domestic violence, bank robbery, mass shooting, or drug trafficking. These are issues that need to be addressed by a country's justice system. But peace and order in any society, while absolutely necessary, are built on the notion of what is just and on justice as a personal virtue.

Notion of Justice

The ancient Greek and Roman philosophers defined *justice* in a single phrase: *suum cuique* ("to each his or her own"). This concept was upheld by Plato, Aristotle, Cicero, Ambrose, Augustine, and especially by Roman law, passing on to become the patrimony of the Western legal tradition. Aquinas referred to the Roman jurist Ulpian to define justice, namely: "Justice is a habit whereby a man renders to each one his due with constant and perpetual will."[2] Its root is the Latin term *ius* which means *right*. Hence, justice seeks to establish what is right, to establish order and equality. Right implies some debt, something owed, an obligation that needs to be met by someone. A just person is one who fulfills his or her duty and sets things right.[3] A just state of affairs means that a relation of equality is observed.

Justice is a stable habit. A person is not really just if he or she occasionally treats other people with fairness. The Angelic Doctor stresses the enduring character of justice, as every moral virtue is meant to be. In itself, the human will tends to seek its own personal interest; we tend to focus on "me," "mine," and "myself," but justice precisely orients the will so that it overcomes this natural, self-serving tendency and opens up to others in a spirit of fair play.[4]

The subject of justice is the will (not the intellect); the virtue inheres in the appetitive (not the cognitive) power. An act of justice is chiefly an act of the will;[5] it is a choice to do the right thing in our social dealings. But make no mistake about it: we are considered just or unjust by what we actually do, not by what we simply plan or intend to do. Justice is not a mere sentiment of benevolence toward others but the actual rendering of what is owed to another. University of Notre Dame ethics professor Jean Porter stresses Aquinas' idea that the just individual not only does what is right but does so knowingly, out of an informed desire to act justly. It implies not merely the tendency to act in accord with the norms of justice but also a stable disposition to care about and pursue right relations. Justice is not a set of abstract principles for social arrangements but is fundamentally a personal virtue.[6]

General Justice

Justice may be considered as a general virtue insofar as it characterizes all the other moral virtues. In this sense, *general justice* is equivalent to moral goodness. The *just* man or woman is a *good* (*holy*) person. St. Joseph, the foster father of Jesus, was a *just man* (Mt 1:19). We do well to always think of other people and consider how our behavior might affect them. The common good is constantly in the mind of a person of integrity. A good teacher, a good doctor, a good father, or a good leader is always understood not in isolation but in relation to a social whole. Even in sport, what defines a good soccer player, for example, is not only dribbling skills but ultimately the capacity for teamwork.

Every human virtue has an aspect of "to others"; it benefits people in general. Every good act has a social dimension, even if it is just a little, discreet effort to control our pride, fear, or curiosity. Virtuous deeds stem from a pure motive, a just will. In effect, the virtue of justice moves the external acts of the other virtues, whose indirect object is the common good. Without an upright intention, what a person does may look praiseworthy, but it is really corrupt at its root. A *harmonious soul* (just person) necessarily helps build a *harmonious polis* (just society).[7]

General justice is also called *common justice* or *legal justice* because one's integrity leads him or her to respect the law. The excellence of justice rests on its social orientation. Justice stands head and shoulders above the other moral virtues since the common good transcends the individual good.[8] Sometimes we need to give up our personal rights in favor of the public interest, as when the state, by eminent domain, expropriates privately owned land to build a railroad or a highway, with just compensation to the property owner. You may find it uncomfortable to go around wearing a face mask, but that's how society thinks it will prevent further spread of a deadly virus. It's not just about you, it's about other people too. The good of one part is subordinate to and forms part of the good of the whole.

The state is a natural institution. It possesses a distinct formal object—the human community ordered toward the common good as such. Hence, general justice represents an authentic form of justice. In the same way that a hand, a head, or a foot defends the whole body-person, so likewise a virtuous citizen defends and promotes the good of his or her body politic, the state. General justice governs the duties of the citizens toward the common good. Its aim is to embody the perfection of the temporal order. Unlike the natural ties that form a family bond, a political community depends on an established order. When each member of the *polis* contributes to the general welfare, it constitutes an act of general justice. How is this concretized? What is the exact obligation of the citizens? The positive law or convention determines the *ad aequalitatem* (equality) that justice requires. Hence, the term *legal justice*.[9]

However, conceptions of justice must strike a proper balance between two extremes: totalitarianism and individualism. While persons are parts of society, it is equally true that no man or woman can be reduced to a mere part of a whole, like a cog in the machine. The subordination of a particular good to the common good does not mean the subordination of the person to society, since the state exists to serve and protect human dignity.[10] Nazi Germany under Adolf Hitler, the Soviet Union under Joseph Stalin, and China under Mao Zedong are typical examples of absolutist and collectivist states that treated their own people as dispensable objects and systematically denied their human rights. In totalitarian regimes, individual rights count for little, whereas those of the state count for everything—a system where justice cannot thrive.

Particular Justice

If there is *general justice* whose object is the common good, there is also *particular justice* whose object is the good of the individual. Since justice is directed to other people, its subject matter is external actions and things,[11] not inner feelings and emotions.

Particular justice deals with divisible and measurable things like property, money, service, titles, and so forth, where one person's gain represents someone else's loss. If you stepped out of a bistro cafe forgetting to pay your bill, it matters little that it was an honest mistake. Injustice was committed (there's at least *material* injustice). Likewise, if a burglar planned to break into a jewelry shop but called it off owing to its heavy security, he or she may have sinned against greed, but not justice, for no external harm was done. In strict justice, what counts is not a person's intention but one's action.

Quasi-Integral Parts

If we take the word justice in the widest sense, a just person is one who simply follows the first moral rule (*synderesis*): "Do good and avoid evil." These dictates of the natural law are requisites of any virtue. But considered as a special virtue, justice is more restrictive and it needs a specific element—to give what is due to another. Hence, the complete formula includes the interpersonal aspect: *to do the good that is due to other people and avoid the evil that harms them and society.*

By doing what is good, a person establishes a certain equality (fair play, due respect, satisfactory service, contract fulfillment, marital fidelity, etcetera); by shunning what is evil, he or she preserves this just state of affairs.[12] Failure to "do good" is *omission* or non-fulfillment of a positive precept ("You shall"). But worse than this is *transgression*, which is a violation of a negative precept to "avoid evil" ("You shall not"). The person who transgresses is not only remiss in his or her duty; he or she does its exact opposite and steps (*graditur*) beyond (*trans*) a fixed boundary set by a precept (natural right, civil law, church norm), making the law an object of contempt.[13] It is already bad enough to evade tax payment (omission), but it is certainly worse to steal and commit fraud (transgression). To ignore one's parents is deplorable, but to insult or hurt them is atrocious.

Both precepts—*do the good that is due to other people and avoid the evil that harms them and society*—are necessary for an act of justice to be perfect, and so they serve as *quasi-integral parts* of justice itself. If one of the two is lacking, justice is rendered imperfect. It is not enough to refrain from causing trouble to other people and to society in general (avoid evil). One must positively give them what they deserve (do good).

Species of Justice (Commutative and Distributive)[14]

Particular justice has two parts. On one hand, justice that governs the mutual dealings of two persons (part to part) is called *commutative justice*, defined as the constant and perpetual will to give to another person his or her strict right, keeping an absolute equality between what is received and what is given.[15] This is justice in the strictest sense; its rules are precise and accurate, as in buying and selling of goods and services: you get your money's worth. Violation of commutative justice demands restitution, an obligation whose gravity depends on the matter involved. Someone who commits a crime must be punished and the victim compensated accordingly. "Without commutative justice, no other form of justice is possible."[16]

On the other hand, justice that regulates the relation of the community to individuals (whole to part) is called *distributive justice*. It is how the burdens and benefits are shared among a class of people with competing needs and claims. More concretely, distributive justice is the constant and perpetual will that inclines the ruler of a group (community) to evenly distribute goods, honors, duties, and penalties among his or her subjects, taking into account each individual's capacity and merits, without forgetting the formal reason for the distribution—the common good. The mean of justice here is proportional (not absolute) equality.[17] Violation of distributive justice imposes an obligation to make proportionate reparation.

Our daily life is affected by how the principles of distributive justice are applied in the place where we live. Political processes are at play. Higher tax rates in New York, for example, are driving businesses out of the Big Apple to relocate to Texas or Florida. When Ivy League universities modify their admission criteria, relying less on SAT or ACT test scores in favor of ethnic diversity, the policy shift affects, one way or the other, every applicant. At some point during the Covid pandemic, health authorities faced the serious dilemma of who should get ventilators and vaccines first, given the relative scarcity of medical supplies.

Public authority has the natural right to demand from citizens whatever is necessary to promote the common good. Such right implies a corresponding civic duty on the part of the subjects to fulfill their obligations toward the state. Every community member ought to share in the task of nation building and social progress as determined by the public policies.[18]

Right: Object of Justice

The object of justice is *right*,[19] what belongs to me, to you, to us, to them, and so forth. *Right* refers to certain things, objects, and actions which a person (physical or juridical) is entitled to have or to do. This is what we mean when we speak of the right to life, work, education, property, wage, or freedom of worship, association, movement, and so forth. If justice inclines us to give to someone what he or she owns, this virtue—taken in the strict sense—is characterized by *aequalitas*, *debitum*, and *alteritas*. Simply stated, justice seeks to establish equality, gives exactly what is due, and is directed to another individual.

Objectivity (*Aequalitas*)

The first essential property of justice is objectivity (*aequalitas*). We can be truly objective only if we can quantify what is owed and what is given. When we talk of justice, we refer to external acts and measurable things. The right of a person (physical or moral) is the yardstick of justice.

In other virtues like fortitude and temperance, the mean of reason (*medio rationis*) is gauged purely by comparison with the person himself or herself, the subject of the passions. The "reasonable" (neither excessive nor deficient) level of patience, courage, anger, and so forth varies from one person to another. What is gluttony for a ballet dancer may not be so for a farmworker. Since it is impossible to quantify passions, we need to discern what constitutes "too much" or "too little" for ourselves.[20]

In contrast, the measure of justice is exactly the thing owed (*medium rei*), the proportion of one thing to another. Justice is perfected by the equality between things and between persons. Equality is the real mean between greater and less.[21] If person X owes one hundred dollars to person Y, then exactly one hundred dollars must be paid by X to Y. While you need to figure out how much to eat or drink at a cocktail party, that kind of problem doesn't exist when you buy a pair of shoes. Just look at the price tag. The real mean (exact value owed) is also the rational mean (reasonable amount to pay), and so justice satisfies the conditions of a moral virtue.

Objectivity is a matter of black and white in commutative justice. It leaves no room for doubt as to how much is due. To *commute* is to change one kind of payment into another and so to interchange. There is strict proportion of equality—*rei ad rem*—between thing and thing (between what is owed and what is paid, between damage and restitution). This is well expressed by the Latin phrase *quid pro quo*—something for something—an exchange of equally valued goods and services. A similar idea is contained in the phrase "tit for tat" (equivalent retaliation). Strict equality is typical of barter trades, contracts, and purchases in which the exact or agreed price is paid, no more or less. If a cashier shortchanges a customer, he or she commits injustice; if the cashier gives him or her extra change or a bonus item like an extra pound of meat or extra piece of apple, that's not strict justice either but an act of liberality.

In addition, other virtues like temperance and fortitude perfect the person only in relation to what befits him or her; the acts of these virtues are just (*right, proper, fitting*) for the individual (*agent*) doing the action. Thus, if you drink one bottle of beer instead of two as an act of sobriety, you foster self-discipline. If your nine-year-old daughter conquers her fear to sleep alone in her bedroom, she becomes a brave girl.

But an act of justice is different due to its radical social orientation; a just person establishes a relation of parity, quite independently of how he or she does it. The object of justice is intrinsically what is due, beyond the rectitude of other virtues.[22] A debtor who settles his or her obligation while inwardly cursing his or her creditor lacks subjective rectitude, but the person's payment is objectively just. One's grudge is not a virtue, but his or her duty to the lender is fulfilled. To further stress this point, when we eat, drink, speak, read, work, dress up, face a problem, or move around, we need to act in a certain way in order to be prudent, brave, or temperate. But when we pay the bills or honor a contract, it does not really matter how we do it as far as justice is concerned. All that is required is that we give to another what he or she has the right to receive.

The first scientific study of "rights" arose in political contexts, born of the need to regulate the mutual relations among members of a community, or between different social groups. Hence, the term *right* has reference to legal juridical orders. But the notion of right goes much deeper than its usage in civil law.

Right is rooted in human nature itself. The most basic philosophical and theological notion of right is eminently personal, not legal. What is due in justice is what belongs to another. Formally, the virtue of justice resides in the will; materially, it governs a person's dealings with other people.

In its deepest meaning, *right* implies a teleological (purpose or end) bond, the direct and exclusive destination of a thing or action (demanded by law or by contract) to a person for his or her use and enjoyment. Anything due to us (payment, salary, good, or service)—anything that we can claim as ours—is meant to help us realize our full human potential.

Consequently, right (what is *suum*) is inalienable and cannot be denied without offending a person's dignity. A despot, a robber, or a swindler may deprive us of what we own or have the right to (for example, free speech, a wallet full of cash, good hotel service), but as Socrates said, the perpetrator of injustice is to be pitied more than his victim. Justice is of such nature that its object, *right*, belongs to a person's true being and, hence, it is inviolable.[23]

Possessives like *mine, yours, ours, theirs, his,* or *her* signify not only an external and causal link between a thing and a person. They indicate *right*, someone's title, possession, authorship, or ownership that other people must recognize and respect. Right precedes justice and is correlative to it, since an act of justice is an act of giving to another his or her due (*suum*). Obligations of justice arise from the existence of rights. No wonder that in *Summa Theologica*, Aquinas tackled the concept of right before the notion of justice as a logical structure.

Obligation (*Debitum*)

The second essential property of justice is the obligation to give what is due. There is a duty to pay, render, compensate, return, or remit exactly what is owed. Logically, this implies the existence of a person's right, which is the origin of another's duty to give. If Peter is indebted to John, what belongs to John (*suum*) gives rise to Peter's obligation (*debitum*) to fulfill. Now what belongs to John is something that he can lay claim to. This introduces us to the notion of *subjective right*, which is the moral faculty or spiritual power of a person to do (freedom to act), to possess (capacity to own), or to demand (ability to claim) what belongs to him or her. Hence, *objective right* (what is due) and *subjective right* (power to demand) are two sides of the same coin. *Subjective right* is not to be understood as sheer physical force or external possession of an object. Rather, it is a moral power that has the force of reason, rooted in natural law. If you are unjustly treated by way of a breach of contract or an unpaid insurance claim, the law, the court, and law enforcement are on your side. A person's moral dominion over a particular good is his or her right, and this is what constitutes the object of justice. We do not refer to false claims or perceived rights, but things and actions that are truly our own. God is the ultimate source of subjective right, who called the human being to participate in the divine government of the world and endowed us with the powers to act in consequence.

One's subjective right is called *active right* (for example, the right to *demand* payment) when it is understood as a person's moral power to claim what belongs to him or her, whereas it is called *passive right* (for example, the right to *be paid* or *receive payment*) when it is taken to mean the action or object the person is entitled to do or own.

The subject of a right can be a *physical person* (an individual, warm body) or a *juridical person* (a corporation or private entity). Never can a human being be treated as an object because nobody on earth can fully and directly own another person.[24] Gone are the days when Western societies maintained slavery as an institution, where people bought and sold other people as if they were pieces of property. The abolitionist movement in Britain in the late eighteenth century to the early nineteenth century was founded on human rights and the Christian faith.

Kinds of Rights

How do people acquire rights? On what ground can we claim this or that to be ours? Or that I am entitled to such and such thing? It is crucial to know the source of rights, be they fundamental rights like life, education, and suffrage, or contingent rights like the right to a free meal and hotel accommodation when your flight is canceled due purely to the airline, or the right to a free warranty service on your new plasma TV or washing machine. Every person has certain goods that are connatural to him or her, while others are acquired or accidental. In varying degrees, they are constituted as objects of one's rights.

Depending on its origin, rights are divided into *natural, divine positive,* and *human* (civil or ecclesiastical). *Natural rights* are those that belong to every person by virtue of the very principles of human nature. The expression *human rights* usually refers to those that are *innate* (inborn, not accorded by the state) and universal (valid across nations and cultures). Every person possesses these rights regardless of race, color, sex, age, religion, or wealth. We have identified some basic human rights in chapter 1, such as the right to life, family, and property; freedom of thought, speech, worship, movement, conscience, association, and standard of living. A second category of natural right that is not inborn is *acquired right*, which as the name suggests, is possessed due to a contingent act, such as inherited land title or ownership of purchased merchandise. Natural rights ought to be protected by human positive laws. A third category of natural right is what the Angelic Doctor calls *ius gentium* or the common right of peoples. It has its origin in the customary law

common to the peoples of the Roman world. Lying between natural law proper and civil law, *ius gentium* is what natural reason
establishes for all mankind. A Roman citizen who is exiled may
lose his or her legal status, but retains his or her right to basic
protection extended to all human beings under *ius gentium*.[25]
These days we often read about refugees crammed on small
wooden boats drifting in the Mediterranean Sea. Obviously they
are illegal migrants, but in the meantime, they have the right to
receive hot food, clothing, and shelter on humanitarian grounds.

Authors dispute what really constitutes the law of peoples,
but the concept is often related to international law, something
to be observed by all peoples.[26]Although a well-developed theory of international law emerged only in the sixteenth century,
especially in the work of the Spanish Dominican Francisco de
Vitoria (c. 1485–1546), the Christian tradition since the seventh
century acknowledged the existence of a *ius gentium*. Its univer-
sality rests on the view that some rights (such as treatment of prisoners of war, safe conduct of diplomats) lie so close to what the
natural law demands that civilized peoples agree that they almost
have the status of natural rights.[27]

Divine positive rights are those rights that a person can demand
thanks to a divine decree, such as the right to hear the gospel
preached, to receive Christian instruction, or to receive the sacra-
ments (such as the Eucharist, penance, or marriage). These rights
are conferred on a person by the express will of God. *Human positive rights* are the ones derived from human laws, either *civil* (a citizen's right to vote, a fair trial, public education, and government
services) or *ecclesiastical* (the right of a Christian faithful to spiritual goods, associations for pious ends, and freedom of inquiry in
a sacred discipline).

Depending on its effects, rights can be either *non-strict*
or *strict*. On the one hand, non-strict rights are rights taken
in a broad sense. They are imperfect rights. Thus, Red Cross

volunteers have the "right" to be recognized for their service. You owe your friend a "debt" of gratitude for lending you his van. The beggar in the subway "ought to" receive alms from the commuters. These are examples of non-strict rights because their violation does not constitute an injustice but only a lack of equity, a certain inconvenience. On the other hand, strict rights are those that are so closely bound to the person that he or she cannot be denied them without causing injury. Contract is a classic example, in which a binding agreement between two parties to the contract are obliged to honor its terms and conditions. Strict rights demand that the aggrieved party must be paid for any damage caused by the non-fulfillment of an obligation.

Depending on its object, strict rights can be further classified into *real rights* (*ius in re*), which refer to rights that are actually possessed, and *personal rights* (*ius ad rem*), which denote rights that are not yet in one's possession. The former implies complete and absolute dominion, while the latter is inchoate and incomplete. A person has a *real right* to the money he or she owns and actually holds, and a *personal right* to the money owed to him or her but not yet in his or her hands. The distinction of concepts is important because while personal right usually leads to real right (I must receive what's destined for me), it does not entitle one to grab it at will, but only to demand its repayment.[28] Strict real right is also called *ownership*, which we shall look at more closely later on.

Otherness (*Alteritas*)

The third essential quality of justice is *alterity* (Latin *alter*, or otherness). The virtue of justice is always directed to another person or entity. If you need money to buy something, you don't borrow cash from yourself and pay yourself later on. Nor can you slander yourself and thereafter file a self-directed libel suit.

If these statements sound odd, it's because there can be no debt to oneself without the subject's knowing and wanting it. As one legal maxim states, *volenti non fit iniuria*—to a willing person, no wrong is done.

We can speak of justice with oneself only in a metaphorical sense, that is, when we do the right thing for ourselves.[29] Statements like, "It's just *right* that you rest well," "You *owe* it to yourself to see a doctor," "It's *proper* that you set boundaries," and "It's quite *fair* that you call for his attention," all mean the "right" thing to do, taking the word *right* in a loose sense.

Justice is possible only when there is "otherness." The virtue governs interpersonal relations. Something is equal, not to itself but to another. Since justice tends to rectify human acts, the otherness it requires must be between distinct individuals (*supposita*) or beings capable of moral actions.

But the mere presence of two individuals does not satisfy the conditions of strict justice, if one of them, in a way, belongs to the other. If your wife takes fifty dollars from your wallet to buy kitchen condiments, she's not exactly stealing; she's getting it from herself somehow, for she's your better half: your consent is presumed. Husband-wife relations are governed by *domestic justice*. If a father enrolls his little boy in a middle school, the kid doesn't acquire strict debt, since he (until he is of age) is part of his dad. Father-child relations are regulated by *paternal justice*. Aquinas also talks about the master-servant relation in which the former has dominion over the latter. This is called *dominative justice*.[30]

In the above cases, there is shared ownership of goods, mitigated "otherness," absence of real *suum* (one's own), or lack of perfect equality, albeit in different degrees. Hence, in the context of a household occupied by a series of dependents, we can only speak of justice in a qualified sense (*secundum quid*), not justice simply (*simpliciter*).[31] To apply the perfect form of justice, we need to find a person who is of equal footing to another person.

Philosophy professor David Gallagher highlights the concept of *civic justice*, where *alteritas* implies citizens of the same body politic who are subjects of the same law under the same authority.[32] Aristotle specifies that "otherness" is not merely "another person," but someone who is not subordinate to the other. Civic justice exists among free and equal (actually or proportionately) persons.[33] It is determined by law that is applied to people of equal juridical status. This means that strict justice can operate only in a political community that is relatively well developed,[34] with an organized judicial system (courts, judges, laws, and so forth).

The Common Good

Given the social nature of the human being, the good of each person is closely related to the common good, defined as the sum total of social conditions which allow people, either as single individuals or as a collective body, to readily flourish and reach their fulfillment.[35] The common good is not the majority vote; it is not about numbers but authentic human values. We are witnesses to how society can generally favor divorce or sanction abortion, but a culture of marital breakups and killing the unborn harm the common good and never foster it.

The notion of the common good has important implications. First, it demands from society *respect for the person* as such, allowing each of us to exercise our natural rights and freedoms needed to realize our vocation. Second, it requires the *social well-being* and *development* of the group itself, including access to food, clothing, health, family, work, education, culture, information, and so on. Finally, the common good presupposes the *peace, security*, and *stability* of a just order.[36]

Every nation has its own peculiar needs that ought to be addressed by the state, whose role it is to promote the common good of the civil society, its citizens, and intermediate bodies.[37]

But we also live in a global village, an interconnected world, a family of nations that calls for a universal common good. Critical issues that involve multiple countries, such as refugees, traffic in narcotics, poverty, nuclear threats, and pandemics, require concerted effort and international cooperation.[38]

Juridical Order and Normative Right

People need to be governed by a legitimate authority whose role is to ensure the common good of society. The human community will be chaotic rather than orderly, unless some individuals are vested with the authority to preserve its institutions and work for everyone's benefit. Even in a classroom setting, until the teacher arrives there tends to be a lot of noise and agitation among the boys and girls. Authority brings order. Human rights can easily be violated without laws that protect them, and precisely the governing authorities are empowered to make (legislate) and enforce (implement) civil laws.

Such authority is rooted in human nature, required by the moral order, and ultimately derived from God. Part of the virtue of justice is the duty that we have as citizens to obey, honor, and respect our political leaders, for as long as they deserve such treatment. If rulers were to enact unjust laws or take measures contrary to the moral order, this would be an abuse of power, a breakdown of authority, and immoral laws do not bind in conscience.

The Angelic Doctor defines law as "an ordinance of reason for the common good, made by him who has care of the community, and promulgated."[39] Therefore, human laws have the character of law only insofar as they conform to right reason. To avoid arbitrary rule, a system of "checks and balances" is applied, where no single government branch wields too much power, and authority is exercised with a sense of responsibility.[40]

While human laws foster certain moral virtues, laws do not have the same scope as the moral order. Legality and morality are two different things. Civil laws govern only external behaviors, those that affect other people, whereas the moral law regulate both acts and intentions, outward conduct and hidden motives. Civil laws seek only to establish order in communal life, while moral law helps us to become virtuous persons. There are traffic rules to be obeyed and tax duties to be fulfilled, but no federal law or city ordinance proscribes laziness or requires purity of heart. Civil laws may vary across space and time, but the moral law is universal and immutable in its fundamental nucleus. Hence, human laws command what is called the ethical minimum (*minimum ethicum*). Still, civil laws that are just must be obeyed, since they oblige in conscience. To the extent that laws promulgated by competent authorities are just, they form part of the moral norm, and they help us attain our final end.

This brings us to the concept of *normative right*, which refers to juridical norms or the set of civil laws that govern interpersonal relations in a given society. The *normative right (right-law)* is what determines, concretizes, enforces, and guarantees the *objective right (what is just, what is due)* of a legal person (physical person or legal entity) which he, she, or it has the power to demand as his, her, or its own (*subjective right*).

Certain actions contrary to moral law are sometimes tolerated by civil laws because worse evils could arise if they were banned. The virtue of prudence precludes the human law from prohibiting all evils. Aquinas states that human law is framed for a group of people, the majority of whom are not perfect in virtue. Thus, human laws do not forbid all vices, which virtuous persons avoid. Civil laws prohibit only the grievous vices: those that cause serious harm to others, those that can be avoided by the majority, those that would lead to the collapse of the community if they were not prevented.[41] Hence, the likes of murder, rape, and theft are criminal offenses.

However, the denial of certain fundamental and inviolable rights like the right to life cannot be tolerated and legitimized. In his encyclical *Evangelium Vitae*, St. John Paul II argues that juridical rulings that permit or legitimize abortion or euthanasia fail to protect equality before the law, militate against the common good, and thus lack authentic juridical validity.[42] Aquinas is clear in pointing out that a law contrary to reason is unjust, and thereby ceases to be a law and becomes an act violence.[43]

Injustice[44]

Any action opposed to the virtue of justice is *injustice*. Otherwise known as *injury* (from *in-iuria*, "violation of a right"), injustice is a moral disorder on two counts. On the one hand, it is a form of contempt of the common good that gives rise to all kinds of aberration. This vice goes against legal justice. Every sin has a character of injustice; there is an element of unfairness in all wicked deeds.[45] No bad action is entirely harmless to others, even if only indirectly. Telling a white lie or arriving late to a meeting may not cause much trouble, but they are unfair.

On the other hand, injustice may refer to a specific vice against particular justice. In this sense, it is the failure to live in right relationship with other people, or the acquired habit of treating others unfairly. The unjust person withholds from other individuals or from the community what he or she ought to give them. Injustice smacks of refusal to recognize people's fundamental equality by denying them what a person himself or herself expects to receive.[46] St. Paul calls *unrighteous* the likes of swindlers, slanderers, thieves, and adulterers (1 Cor 6:9–10), who shall be excluded from God's kingdom.

When we face some kind of injustice, a set of rules can help us determine what exact violation is done, how serious is the harm, how guilty is the offender, and what sort of recompense is due.

The first rule is that every act of injustice, every injury inflicted on another person, is mortal sin *ex genere suo*; that is, it can be venial if the act is imperfect (due to lack of advertence or lack of full consent) or if the matter involved is light. It is not always easy to figure out what constitutes a light or a grave matter. Stealing a dollar from a billionaire is wrong, but it would not harm him or her as much as it would hurt a street beggar if the latter were the victim. In principle, when a significant harm is done to a person or the common good, when the offense is blatant, when the injury is fiercely opposed by the aggrieved parties, we have a case of grievous injustice.[47] Even if the unjust act strictly violates only commutative justice, as when a passenger gets out of a taxi without paying, he or she harms the common good and disturbs communal peace. Anything unfair and dishonest is injurious to the social whole.

The second rule is that not all unjust acts are the same, and they are classified according to their moral objects. Calumny, forgery, homicide, and pilferage are all acts of injustice, but not of the same kind. Murder is far different from fraud both in the type and gravity of offense. Hence, one must know the species of an unjust act in order assess its moral value. The second rule answers the question, "What exactly happened?"; "What was the crime committed?"; or "What did that crook do to you?" It is not the motive that we are after here, but the specific nature of the offense.

Aristotle said that a person may do an unjust thing without being unjust.[48] This sounds strange, but he makes an interesting point, which is the third rule: No one is guilty of an injustice unless he or she wills it. A person who inadvertently violates another's right commits but *indirect* or *material injustice*, not *formal* or *direct injustice.* If you lose your brakes as you bike down the road, hitting a mobile hotdog stand and hurling down the footlongs and ketchup bottles, there is a material (but not a formal) offense. After all, you did not do it on purpose. Of course, you should apologize and perhaps pay for the damage, although restitution is not always morally required in material injustice, as we shall see later on.[49]

As a corollary to the preceding rule, no person suffers injustice if he or she wants it, as mentioned earlier. An act that is objectively offensive ceases to be so if the supposed victim does not oppose it. If a stranger tries to grab your handbag and you let him or her do so, offering no resistance at all, you are not being wronged, technically. If a squatter builds a structure on the vacant lot of his or her neighbor and the latter condones it, in a way, no injustice is committed. Right or ownership depends on one's free will, so no inequality happens if a person forfeits something voluntarily.[50] By consenting to the perpetrator of injustice, you effectively free him or her from moral responsibility—so long as you truly tolerate the act, that is, without your being forced, coerced, or deceived.

But there is a limit to the scope of willful consent to injustice. The above rule does not apply to *inalienable rights* (rights that cannot be licitly given up). The doctor who helps a patient to commit suicide upon the latter's request is morally culpable, precisely because no person can lawfully renounce his or her right to life. The informed, legal, written consent of the patient and his family does not exonerate the assisting physician from moral liability. Similarly, a husband cannot voluntarily renounce his conjugal right by tolerating the adulterous affair of his wife. His ridiculous consent, if real, does not justify the injustice of marital infidelity. We cannot give free consent to an injustice if the matter involved is a human right that cannot be transferred or surrendered.

Social Injustice

Social injustice is a situation in which the rights of a person or group of people are not respected. There is unequal treatment of equals, or equal treatment of unequals, shown for example, in racial discrimination, economic inequality, unfair labor practices, or suppression of legitimate freedoms. We tend to appreciate the importance of justice more if *our* rights are violated, as when we are victimized by a scam (commutative justice) or we are overtaxed by the government (distributive justice).

The prevalence of injustice in society gives rise to so-called *structures of evil*. Corruption, abortion, drug trafficking, and the like are not just development flaws, psychological weaknesses, simple mistakes, or the results of a defective system.[51] These are communal situations and institutional structures that are the fruits of the sins of men and women.[52] Social injustice is nothing other than an aggregate of unjust acts of individuals.

Violence almost always erupts when rights, especially fundamental human rights, are violated. Major world conflicts, political agitations, and social unrest flare up for this reason. History is replete with examples of how, in the face of injustices, people clamor for change, such as the civil rights movement in the United States, the peace crusade of Mahatma Gandhi in India, the abolition of apartheid in South Africa, the collapse of the Iron Curtain in Eastern Europe, the battle for democracy in Myanmar, and the pro-democracy protests in China, to name a few. These are landmark struggles for human freedom in the face of oppression, popular revolts to reclaim what has been unduly usurped.

Literature often serves as a critique of societal malaise. Charles Dickens' *Oliver Twist* (1838) was a social novel that satirized child labor, domestic violence, and poverty in England during the Industrial Revolution. Victor Hugo's historical novel

Les Misérables (1862) emphasized the themes of love, mercy, dignity, hope, and redemption in the context of the July 1830 Revolution in Paris amidst economic inequality, disease, food shortage, and joblessness. Hugo wrote in his novel, "First problem: To produce wealth. Second problem: To share it,"[53] and he also said, "He who opens a school door, closes a prison."[54]

Social injustice is at its worst when it is state-sponsored. The major political and social upheavals have a characteristic pattern: the systematic denial of basic human rights by state authorities or the occupying power, and the subsequent mass mobilization—peaceful or violent—to overthrow the dominant forces and install a regime of change and equality. It is in the nature of the person to defend what is naturally his or hers.

Restitution[55]

Restitution is the act of restoring to a former state or position. It is an act of commutative justice by a person who possesses what belongs to another, either because the latter allowed it (such as loan or deposit) or because it was forcibly taken from him or her (such as robbery or fraud). To restore is to reinstate someone in the dominion of his or her thing, so that equality is re-established. In other words, to make up for a violated right.

Our lives are so intertwined that restitutions are quite common. If the pizza you ordered turns up hard, dry, and moldy, you will naturally complain and demand to have it replaced or get a full refund. Landlords deduct portions of the security deposit to cover the cost of damages caused by tenants in the apartments they occupy. Amusement parks like Tokyo Disneyland, Universal Orlando Resort, or Copenhagen Tivoli Gardens pay damages if ride accidents occur due to negligence or lack of safety protocols.

But it is not always possible to return exactly what has been taken away, either because of the nature of the object or because it was simply lost. Thus, the notion of restitution is widened to include *compensation* or *reparation* for the damages inflicted. Permanent loss of vision due to an error in eye surgery is an example of irreparable damage. One's eyesight cannot be restored, no matter how much compensation is paid. A person who is the target of media bashing has his or her good reputation tarnished in a way that cannot be totally restored.

It is useful to distinguish between *restitution*, which is returning the object taken or its material equivalent, and *satisfaction*, which concerns the person and is aimed at repairing a good name that has been ruined. *Satis facere* (to do enough) means to restore a person's good reputation (to the extent possible) through public retraction. To indemnify the harm done, the author of the libel backs off from his or her false statements or does equivalent forms of restorative justice to the extent possible.

The duty of restitution arises especially from violations of commutative justice, which demands a perfect equality between what is taken and what is lost, between the damage and the reparation.[56] Commutative justice protects individual rights. It preserves the natural and relative independence of the human person. In our social life and mutual relations, each of us enjoys a juridical sphere that delineates our property rights, which we all need in order to live in freedom and dignity. Violating this independence per se is a grave disorder against our neighbor.

Any act of injustice is at once a juridical offense and a moral disorder, a crime, and a sin. When reparation is made, equality is restored, but the offender may still be punished by law. When a thief is caught, he or she is not off the hook after returning what was stolen; the culprit is also punished for the crime of larceny. Countries and states impose different penalties, but depending on the gravity (misdemeanor, fraud, embezzlement, robbery, or grand theft) they often involve a fine, probation, or imprisonment. Civil laws normally adopt the basic principle that the aggrieved party has the right to exact restitution of the things he or she was unjustly deprived of, plus compensation for the damages suffered.

Every unjust act that causes injury to another person and violates his or her rights constitutes *unjust damage*. This can be *personal damage* (harm to life, limb, liberty, reputation) or *real damage* (extrinsic to the person like property). Unjust damage that is *formal* (known and intended as such) and *real* (effectively causes injury) requires restitution. No restitution is needed if the damage is *involuntary* or merely *material*. An act that is not intentional does not entail moral responsibility. Nevertheless, a judge may order compensation for the damage. Civil law can reasonably demand restitution, if only to foster the common good and urge people to be more careful in their actions.[57] Thus, in the above example of a hotdog kiosk that a bicycle rider hits accidentally, restitution is not morally due, but still, it can mean paying a property-damage liability in civil law.

Having analyzed the notions of justice, right, injustice, and restitution, we shall now discuss specific human rights. This book is not the venue to explain all the possible rights, but we shall tackle three major areas: 1) *right to life and bodily integrity*; 2) *right to the truth and good reputation*; and 3) *right to ownership and private property*.

Right to Life and Bodily Integrity (Corporal Goods)

Foremost among the basic human rights is the right to life, obviously, since a dead person cannot enjoy any right at all. *"Human life is sacred* because from its beginning it involves the creative action of God and it remains forever in a special relationship with the Creator, who is its sole end."[58] The United

States Declaration of Independence states that "all men are created equal, that they are endowed by their Creator with certain unalienable Rights, that among these are Life, Liberty and the pursuit of Happiness."[59]

The right to life and bodily integrity is protected by the fifth commandment: "You shall not kill" (Ex 20:13). This precept gives rise to two fundamental principles: 1) The life of the innocent is inviolable and hence, *abortion, homicide, suicide,* and *euthanasia* are gravely immoral; and 2) The life of a guilty man or woman cannot be taken except in the case of *self-defense, just war,* and the *death penalty*.[60] We shall now briefly discuss each of these cases.

Homicide: *Homicide* is any action that directly causes the death of another person. Direct and intentional killing is gravely contrary to human dignity and harms the common good. This is a universal prohibition that obliges everyone, anywhere and anytime.[61] It is never lawful to slay an innocent and righteous individual.[62] "Whoever sheds the blood of man, by man shall his blood be shed; for God made man in his own image" (Gn 9:6). When the person killed is a close relative, the crime is *parricide* and this circumstance aggravates the moral offense.

The right to life demands respect for bodily integrity, and so anything that inflicts undue physical harm is gravely wrong. *Kidnapping* and *hostage taking* bring on a reign of terror that subjects the victims to threats and tremendous pressures. *Terrorism* uses force or violence to achieve certain objectives, with indiscriminate killings of innocent civilians. *Torture* employs physical or moral violence to extract confessions, inflict punishment, scare opponents, or satisfy plain hatred. All of these violate the right to life and physical integrity. In the same vein, *amputation, mutilation,* and *sterilization* of innocent people are unethical, except if these are done strictly for therapeutic reasons.[63]

Abortion: If it is gravely unjust to kill an innocent person, no one is more innocent and defenseless than the unborn child. Thus, *abortion*[64] that is procured or directly willed either as an end or as a means is a serious violation of the right to life. For every person possesses the inviolable rights of a human being. Life is sacred and must be protected and cared for in all its stages, from conception to natural death, from cradle to grave. Expulsion from the womb of an immature, nonviable fetus is induced abortion, a form of murder. We do not refer to miscarriage: that is quite common and to the extent that it is unprovoked, it is called spontaneous abortion. The evil of procured abortion lies precisely in the intention to terminate human life.

So-called "reproductive freedom" (that is, a woman's right over her sexual life and reproductive health) is a classic example of a false right that is based on the wrong assumption that a woman can dispose of the baby in her womb as if it were something (an object), not someone (a human life). Civil laws that allow abortion or, worse, oblige others to condone an intrinsically evil action, are manifestly unjust. Legislation that requires hospitals and clinics to admit abortion providers (to women who request it) is immoral and must be opposed on constitutional grounds and by way of conscientious objection. Doctors, anesthesiologists, nurses, midwives, and so forth who find themselves in situations of having to assist in abortion are morally obliged to have recourse to objection of conscience. Laws are binding only if they promote the common good of the person, not destroy him or her. The right to life is a constitutive element of civil society.

Self-defense: In an act of *self-defense*, a person can deal a lethal blow to an unjust aggressor. Love toward oneself (upright self-love) is a fundamental moral principle; thus, any man or woman who is attacked has the right and even the duty to repel the assailant, to defend him- or herself, and to protect the lives of other people. In a sense, the violent and unjust aggressor who attempts to inflict serious harm on others loses his or her right to life. Bank robbers and home intruders who are killed by their would-be victims are responsible for their own deaths since they provoked their tragic end. A typical example is a restaurant owner in York, Pennsylvania, who shot and killed a man who attempted to rob him at gunpoint. The district attorney's office and the police department did not press charges on the restaurant owner after investigation showed it was a "justifiable homicide." Whoever defends his or her life is not guilty of murder. However, legitimate self-defense requires the use of proportionate means to avert the attack, applying just enough force to disable the criminal and if possible, avoid the person's death.[65] If a would-be victim repeatedly shoots a person trying to grab his or her bicycle, that reaction may be "overkill" that goes way beyond legitimate self-defense.

Death Penalty: The common good requires peace and order. When the people's security is threatened, the public authority can use arms to repel any aggressor against the civil community. News reports of mass shootings, bank heists, and a spate of rapes hit the headlines once in a while. The state can and must curb the spread of behavior detrimental to people's rights and the basic rules of civil society. One way to redress the offense and correct the criminal is recourse to the *death penalty*. Following a fair trial, *capital punishment* may be an appropriate response to certain grave crimes. In recent years, the Catholic Church has worked for the worldwide abolition of the death penalty in view of the increasingly effective systems of detention and the idea of giving the guilty a chance of redemption.[66] Still, justice requires punishment and reparation for the harm done and the protection of society from future threats.

Suicide: Killing an innocent person is gravely unjust. But what about taking one's own life? Is there an injustice involved in *suicide*, which is voluntary by definition? To answer this question, we need to realize that a person has a useful or indirect ownership of his or her body, but not absolute ownership. We own our body but under the law of God, for every person belongs to him. "None of us lives to himself; and none of us dies to himself." (Rom 14:7–8; see Wis 16:13). Related to suicide is *euthanasia*, otherwise known as *mercy killing* or *assisted suicide*, which is intentional killing upon request by the handicapped, sick, or dying. It is gravely contrary to human dignity.

Unless the person concerned is mentally deranged, suicide is always a serious moral disorder.[67] The Angelic Doctor argues in favor of life, saying that a person ought to love and preserve him- or herself. We are naturally inclined to protect our health and resist bodily corruption. Life may be harsh and burdensome, but life is still a priceless gift. "La vita è bella"—life is wonderful, as they say in Italian. Taking one's own life is contrary to the human good. But since every individual is part of a community, we also owe it to others to preserve our existence as much as we can. Whoever commits suicide in an act of despair not only harms him- or herself, but also injures social life. Finally, ending one's own life goes against God because life is God's blessing and is subject to his power. The Lord alone can pronounce sentence of life and death (Dt 32:39).[68]

There is nothing wrong with using analgesics, narcotics, and other drugs to alleviate pain, even if these indirectly shorten a patient's life. What is evil is intentional killing, which includes the omission of the logical and effective means to preserve health. However, no one is obliged to resort to costly and extraordinary artificial means to prolong vegetative life when there is no hope of recovery.[69] It makes little sense to sell one's property and spend enormous amounts of money to extend for one more day the life of a terminally ill patient. That is overzealous treatment of a hopeless case.

Just War: Nobody wins in a war; everybody stands to lose. Armed conflicts represent a dismal failure in human relations. War is a senseless way to resolve conflicts and often takes a heavy death toll, tears apart the economic fabric of entire nations, and causes serious psychological traumas to children and families. The Second Vatican Council stressed the need to avoid war as much as possible, denouncing the use of weapons of mass destruction.[70]

However, every nation has the right to legitimate defense against an unjust aggressor. Under certain conditions, a government can launch a military campaign to defend its population and sovereignty, invoking its *ius ad bellum* (war decision right). *Just war* is licit if there is glaring injustice that needs to be corrected (the principle of just cause); all peaceful and diplomatic means have been exhausted (the principle of last resort); the military action has a reasonable chance of success (the principle of success); the legitimate authority alone decides if war is justified (the principle of public authority); all evil intentions are excluded (the principle of rightful intention); noncombatants are not to be targeted (the principle of discrimination); and finally, no more force than necessary is employed to defeat the enemy and vindicate the just cause (the principle of proportionality).

Once war has broken out, it must be waged in keeping with the *ius gentium* and the rules of war (International Humanitarian Law or IHL) set out by the Geneva Conventions. Known as *ius in bello*, these are a series of treaties that define the methods of warfare as well as the treatment of civilians, prisoners of war (POW), and soldiers rendered *hors de combat* (unable to fight). IHL applies to the belligerent parties and is designed to save lives, reduce suffering, and respect human dignity. If the rules of war are violated, the guilty party or parties (not excluding individuals) can be prosecuted in the international courts and suffer the consequences of their war crimes. For example, the late Yugoslav President Slobodan Miloševic went on trial in 2002 in The Hague, Netherlands, on charges of genocide and war crimes in Bosnia, Croatia, and Kosovo.

The justness of a war is a matter of general justice and is beyond the realm of commutative justice. Hence, soldiers have no direct responsibility for armed conflicts. When deployed, the soldiers gear up, ready their weapons, pack their rucksacks, bring photos of their loved ones, and perhaps take a little prayer book, but sometimes they don't even know their exact mission initially. As a general rule, a combatant who in good faith takes part in a just war is allowed to use whatever force is necessary to quash enemy resistance, as long as his means are not intrinsically evil and he observes the rules of war.

Sexual Violence: Rape is the forcible violation of the sexual intimacy of another person. A grave act of injustice and sin against charity, rape deeply wounds the respect, freedom, and physical and moral integrity of its hapless victim,[71] whether a man or a woman. But there are other forms of sexual violence, such as forced sex between intimate partners, sexual harassment, forced prostitution, sexual trafficking, coerced incest, and sexual abuse of minors. All sexual offenses are intrinsically evil acts; they are never justifiable. Coercion may involve blackmail, threat, or intimidation. Sexual assault has a profound and lasting impact on physical and mental health, not to mention the fact that victims are often stigmatized and ostracized by their families and others.

In many parts of the world, there are well-documented cases of migrant women forced into sexual acts as a condition to cross borders . Or they can be deceived into believing they are obtaining work in a service or domestic industry, only to end up in brothels where their passports are confiscated. Sexual assault may also happen to people in police custody or in prison. Rape victims often grapple with pain and shame, and if they do not speak up, they are deprived of the necessary help like counseling, the rapist goes scot-free, and justice is not vindicated.

Bioethics: Bioethics covers a broad range of issues like reproductive technologies, sexuality, and end-of-life practices, but we shall focus on two specific areas: *embryonic stem cell* studies and *in vitro fertilization* (IVF).

Biomedical sciences have led to embryonic stem cell research, which involves artificial interventions into human life in its incipient stages. Scientists experiment on human embryos in order to treat the likes of Parkinson's disease, arthritis, stroke, spinal cord injury, or even skin wrinkles. Embryonic stem cell studies involve the destruction of embryos, a gravely immoral act. Biotech experts use cloning to produce embryos in order to harvest stem cells. This is an attempt by humanity to have absolute dominion over nature. It is never licit to manipulate the biological process and terminate life in order to save other lives.[72] The end does not justify the means.

Unregulated clinics are sprouting up all over the world that may not only fail to deliver but may even put their patients at great risk. Reports abound of stem cell treatments that actually led to bad outcomes like lesions or tumors. Yet the more serious issue here is not medical but ethical. Human life is sacred and a person's dignity is inviolable.

Closely related to the stem cell issue is in vitro fertilization (IVF), which is a process of fertilizing an egg (ovum) by combining it with a male sperm in a glass (in vitro). This procedure involves stimulating a woman's ovulatory process, removing ova from her ovaries, and letting a man's sperm fertilize them in a culture medium in a laboratory (artificial insemination). A fertilized egg or *zygote* is then implanted in a uterus to initiate a pregnancy. Leftover embryos that are not implanted are frozen in liquid nitrogen. Sometimes, the implantation is done in a surrogate mother's uterus. The ban of IVF in some countries gave rise to what is called "fertility tourism," which is traveling to another country where IVF is legal.

IVF violates human dignity, for it treats the baby as a product subject to manipulation, violating the child's integrity as a human being with an immortal soul from the moment of conception.[73] We are supposed to be the fruit of the conjugal love of our parents, not the product of a test-tube process. It is never morally licit to separate the conception of a human being from the marital act of husband and wife, the procreative aspect from the unitive aspect of marriage. Embryo banks are proliferating where anyone can "buy a baby" using a credit card, giving the "parent" the option to pick a genetic source who is smart, handsome, or pretty, with blonde hair and blue eyes. Society is so keen on protecting the rights of men and women, but we forget that the unborn child, created in the *image and likeness of God*, has inherent human rights that should not be violated.

Organ Transplant:

> "*Organ transplants* are in conformity with moral law if the physical and psychological dangers and risks to the donor are proportionate to the good sought for the recipient. Organ donation after death is a noble and meritorious act and is to be encouraged as an expression of generous solidarity."[74] However, the donor or his or her proxy must give explicit consent. St. John Paul II affirmed that organ donation, done in an ethically proper way, is a beautiful act of expressing the culture of life with a view to offering a chance of health and even life itself to the sick who sometimes have no other hope of survival.[75]

Obviously, it is gravely unjust to remove surgically the heart of a man who is still alive in order to save someone badly in need of a heart transplant. A human organ is useful if it is not a dead tissue, so its donor has to be a person whose brain has irreversibly ceased to function (brain death) but whose organs can still be kept functioning through mechanical means. Once again, it is never licit to kill an innocent life in order to save another.

Right to the Truth and a Good Reputation (Spiritual Goods)

Every person has the right to the truth. None of us likes to be deceived. The eight commandment forbids lying, thus: "You shall not bear false witness against your neighbor" (Ex 20:16). As stated earlier, *sincerity* resembles *justice* since it is directed to another person and a certain equality is established when we are honest with other people. In other words, a person who is sincere is being fair with everyone. But while justice implies a *strict right*, sincerity involves but a *moral right*. Even so, language can promote or damage a person's honor and good reputation.[76]

Respect for the person implies the proper use of the written or spoken word. We all have the right to free speech, but not at the expense of another's good name. The right to the truth is violated in many ways (such as through lying, rash judgment, suspicion, boasting, flattery, adulation), but we shall focus on the use of language that harms one's honor and good name, and therefore demands reparation. In his treatise on justice, Aquinas tackles five common verbal injuries: *reviling, backbiting, tale-bearing, derision,* and *cursing.*

Reviling (vituperation) is speaking against a person to his or her face. It is an open, loud, and injurious verbal attack against one's honor, although deeds and signs may be employed. Honor is the respect and recognition of a man or a woman's worth or excellence, the social witness given to human dignity to which each of us has the natural right.[77] To revile is to do the opposite, that is to say, shame and disgrace the person right up front. When we are insulted, the affront we suffer is a violation of our honor called *contumely*. Often, fits of anger and heated arguments lead to scornful remarks and abusive language. Whoever hurls insults is obliged to make reparation. If the offense happens in public, the restitution must also be made in public. Political leaders sometimes deliver speeches or send tweets laden with insults and name-calling to humiliate their opponents. Partisan politics is not a license to tirade and verbal abuse.

If *reviling* is a frontal attack against one's honor, backbiting (defamation) is to bite from behind, causing harm to one's good name or reputation.[78] These two vices resemble stealing of external goods. Like reviling, robbery is open and violent; like backbiting, theft is secret and quiet. Speaking ill of a person behind his or her back (with full knowledge and full consent) on a serious matter is a grave injustice. If someone defames another in our presence, we should try not to listen or attempt to change the topic, reminding the fellow that it is not fair to put someone in a bad light. We do have the moral duty to correct the backbiter and not tolerate such injustice out of fear or false human respect.[79] Silence in this case can be a form of tacit consent and passive complicity.

Reputation is the common opinion about the good character of a person, the fruit of one's meritorious activity. It is like a property earned through good deeds and personal excellence. To despoil another's reputation without due cause is an act of *defamation*. Also known as *denigration* (from *denigrare*, to blacken), it refers to any action that unjustly tarnishes, sullies, or detracts from the good name that a person has enjoyed up until then. Even a dead person in principle retains the right to good reputation.[80]

Essential to the notion of *defamation* is the lack of just cause or valid reason to destroy a person's public esteem. Whoever exposes a hidden crime so that its perpetrator may be prosecuted is not guilty of defamation. Sometimes it is necessary to spill the beans when the common good requires it. In order to defend oneself, a person may also reveal the hidden faults of his or her neighbor.[81] If you see a man tampering with an ATM machine, it is not defamation to tip off the police. If your sister is dating a man whom you know to be a scammer and gambling addict, she deserves to know.

Save for these exceptions, it is never licit to cast aspersions on someone. If we have knowledge of a person's secret failings, we are not entitled to broadcast this sensitive information, any more than we want anyone to disclose our hidden sins. *Simple defamation* or *detraction* is the technical term for the act of revealing a person's unknown but real defects. *Detraction* is an offense against charity and justice, not because the detractor makes up stories, but because there is no reason to tarnish our neighbor's good reputation, even if he or she does not deserve it. The hatred, discord, and grudges stirred up by detraction also disturb social harmony.

What if the person being talked about is a Hollywood celebrity or a senator? If his or her defects, failures, or crimes are already known by many people, can we licitly join the chatter? A good rule of thumb is to ask ourselves: "What do we get from the rumor mill?" In principle, we have the duty to refrain from spreading further the negative publicity without serious cause. Gossip serves no useful purpose; it is always an imperfection, a cause of moral disorders, and a sin against charity.[82]

If the defamation involves a lie, if a person makes false accusations, we have a case called *slander* or *calumny*. *Slander* is a baseless charge, making it more serious than detraction. Remarks contrary to the truth about a person mislead other people to judge him or her falsely. It is already bad enough to become the object of detraction (someone discloses our faults to others); it is even worse to suffer calumny (someone heaps up lies to smear our good name). If you happen to know that your friend or colleague is an illegitimate child, flunked the board exam, or spent a night in jail, you have no reason to divulge this truth. Even less reason do you have to maliciously share these stories if they never really happened.

Tale-bearing is similar to backbiting since both are secret and quiet verbal attacks. The two terms are often taken as synonymous and may also be considered *gossip*. The subtle difference according to the Angelic Doctor is that tale-bearing is meant to sever friendships, whereas backbiting is intended to ruin a person's good name. The tale-bearer speaks ill of someone to stir the minds of his neighbors, pitting one person against another, and thus sowing discord and contentions.[83] In real life, of course, the two effects often go together: tarnished name and social alienation. In whatever form, gossip can ruin people's lives. Gossips thrive on a willing audience, so we must try to break the chain, saying something like, "I'm sorry, I don't really feel comfortable talking about people if they're not here to tell their side of the story."

Derision is intended to shame a person by making fun of him or her. It is done in jest, through scornful laughter at another's failings and defects. *Derision* makes a person despicable and the offense is more serious the more respect the person deserves. To ridicule a loafer and scalawag is not the same as to ridicule a city official or church pastor. Sometimes it is just a humorous sarcasm or playful mockery, but it can include formal contempt. Aquinas says that *derision* is all the more grievous to the extent that it takes people away from good deeds.[84] People who laugh at others' failures are mean-spirited; they feel superior by putting others down. Derision is clearly a form of injustice.

Finally, there is cursing (*maledictio*), which is either efficacious, when a person imprecates or asks God to cause evil to befall someone, or inefficacious, when it is merely an expression of desire. To curse God is irreverence and hatred of the Divinity. To curse persons, especially those who are consecrated, is *blasphemy*, insofar as they are the handiwork of God. Cursing and swearing are often born of impatience: they are little frustrations or outburst of anger over petty annoyances,[85] as when a car cuts you off, or you smash your finger, or someone cuts in line. In some circles profanity and expletives no longer sound vulgar but are part of everyday speech. Yet the f-word and s-word are not just words; they reveal something about us and how sensitive we are to other people's feelings. What we say affects our relationships. We tend to lose the respect and esteem of our friends if we habitually use foul language. "Good" thing if we swear only at the bad weather or heavy traffic; what if we curse someone who angers us? It is a form of verbal abuse.

A public statement contrary to the truth takes on particular gravity. In court it is called *false witness*. When made under oath, it becomes perjury.[86] An oath is an invocation to God to witness the truth of a statement. But the falsehood inherent in perjury annuls the purpose of the oath.[87] What distinguishes perjury from a simple lie is that the former is under strict obligation to bear witness to the truth. Civil laws vary in different places, but generally a witness in a trial commits perjury when he or she knowingly and intentionally lies about a material issue.

Reparation of Verbal Injuries

Just how serious is the evil of a defamatory utterance? How much harm does it cause? The answer depends on a series of elements, namely: 1) the *defamator*: accusations lodged by a dignitary like a congressman have a lot more weight than those raised by a wicked person whom nobody takes seriously; 2) the *victim*: the excellence of the person charged is also relevant. To claim that "the cab driver was caught driving drunk" is not as grave as to say that "the state governor was caught driving drunk;" 3) the *audience*: character assassination that is heard or read by hundreds of people is certainly worse than what reaches the ears of just a handful of individuals. It matters too, whether the audience are rumormongers or a discreet and highly educated crowd; and lastly 4) the *motive*: slander is always wrong since its motive can never be good.[88]

The moral evil of defamation does not change with the kind of vice imputed to a person (he is a liar, he is incompetent, he takes advantage of others). But the gravity of the accusation matters. Charges of tardiness are not the same as charges of murder. It is a lot more serious to be accused of extortion of funds than to be blamed for tracking mud into the house.

Restitution is done when the culprit retracts or takes back his or her harmful words. This is not as easy as making up for damage to property. One can easily return a stolen bicycle or restructure an unpaid loan, but it is almost impossible to restore a person's good name once it is tarnished. In the case of detraction, where what is said is true but should not have been spread, we cannot reverse the statement by claiming that it was untrue. That would be a lie. But the author of defamation must try his or her best to repair the damage caused, by apologizing and praising the qualities of the person he or she had previously defamed.[89] If we are the sad victim of defamation, we have the right to demand reparation, even if we forgive our detractor.

Whether it be material (*restitution*) or moral (*satisfaction*) in form, the reparation must be evaluated in terms of the extent of the damage inflicted. This is a duty that obliges in conscience.[90] Sometimes, *calumny* has consequences in terms of material loss, not just tainted reputation. When I was studying in Rome back in the late 1990s, a popular bakery and pastry chain suffered huge losses in sales when a disgruntled client spread the false news that a panettone (sweet dough studded with candied fruits and raisins) he bought from the pastry shop contained a piece of broken glass. A smear campaign like this can ruin not just one's good name but also one's business.

In civil law, *slander* usually refers to verbal defamation (uttered by the defendant), whereas *libel* is a written or published defamatory statement. It is important to know the rules about who can say what without getting into legal hot water, as well as to learn what a plaintiff needs to prove in order to hold someone liable for defamation.[91] Basic knowledge of defamation lawsuits can put us on guard against committing slander (wittingly or unwittingly), and can help us defend ourselves against defamatory statements made in person, online, or via social media.

Your name is not an empty tag, random identification, or set of hollow words. Your name is yourself; it carries your honor and represents your dignity. Your name is linked to your personality, achievements, fame, purpose, legacy, and so forth. In the Bible, names have deep meaning, for they convey a person's identity and mission. If a long-lost friend still remembers your name, you appreciate it. If you hear your name praised, the whole of "you" is being honored. Therefore, your name is important in your life and relationships.

Naturally we feel offended if our name is maligned. We do not just smile and shrug off the disparagement. Sometimes, it is enough to be misquoted to be blacklisted and lose friends. But just as we would not allow anybody to tarnish our good name, we must also be careful not to defame other people. Not everything that pops into our head needs to be verbalized. Before we blurt out something, we should think of how it might affect others. If we cannot say anything nice about a person, we had better stay quiet. There are trivial lies about small matters, the so-called "white lies" told to avoid an inconvenience or an embarrassment, but that do not really damage another's good reputation. But quite another thing are defamatory words that injure a person's honor. "For every kind of beast and bird, of reptile and sea creature, can be tamed and has been tamed by humankind, but no human being can tame the tongue—a restless evil, full of deadly poison. With it we bless the Lord and Father, and with it we curse men" (Jas 3:7–9).

The Mass Media

Between the media and its readers there exists a sacred, invisible bond founded on honesty. It is a unique kind of public trust. Writers, broadcasters, publishers, and producers aim to get a fair share of the market by winning public confidence and support. Those of us who read, listen, and watch naturally expect quality news, accurate data, enlightening views, and sound opinions. Distortion of the truth betrays the public trust and defeats the media's *raison d'être*.

People have the fundamental right to true information, which is not a commodity but a social good. It deals with ethical concepts like freedom, objectivity, truth, honesty, and privacy.[92] As a rule of thumb, the media fulfills its social function when it seeks the good of the human person and of society,[93] whereas anything that degrades human dignity is professional malpractice.

Some people read newspapers and watch TV to get informed; others do it as a form of entertainment—to experience vicarious joy, nail-biting suspense, or to satisfy curiosity.

But regardless of their motives, readers and viewers expect to get reliable information. Media critics have observed the growing

> emphasis in the mainstream media on tabloidization, infotainment and journalistic subjectivity. 'Facts' and 'information' give way to 'feelings,' with 'hard' news being replaced by endless 'soft,' human interest, sensational stories, often based on unacceptable invasions of privacy.[94] *Time* magazine claimed that "stories, whether obtained by fair means or foul, are routinely embellished. . . . Tabloid culture rarely distinguishes between the public interest and what interests the public.[95]

The journalist is accountable not just to his or her editor or publisher but above all to the public. Hence, he or she must work with integrity, shunning bribery, refusing to kowtow to power pressures and intent on promoting the common good.[96] Press freedom can never be a license to defame, calumniate, or slander. There is always a need to purify the *word* (oral or written) of any misrepresentation and deception, and to restore its original function: as a carrier of the truth and a vehicle of understanding between individuals and peoples.

Right to Ownership and Private Property (External Goods)

The seventh commandment declares, "You shall not steal" (Ex 20:15). It forbids taking or keeping unjustly the goods of other people, or causing them harm with respect to their possessions. Implied in this precept of the Decalogue is the right to private property, which is a fundamental human right. Within proper limits, people need to own certain things in order to survive and live in freedom and dignity. The miseries of the poor, homeless, and dispossessed only highlight the need for all men and women to have at least the basic needs like food, clothing, and shelter.

But how do people acquire property? What are the criteria for the distribution of goods? How much should you own and who determines it? We begin by stating the principle of the universal destination of the earth's resources: *The goods of creation are destined for the whole of mankind.* This is primordial. "Goods of production—material or immaterial—such as land, factories, practical or artistic skills, oblige their possessors to employ them in ways that will benefit the greatest number."[97] On their part, the end users and consumers should enjoy the goods with moderation, ready to help the needy in a spirit of human solidarity.[98]

We own real estate, lay claim to properties, hold legal titles, guard certain valuables, or secure our savings. Yet human beings do not have absolute dominion over material things but only stewardship, for God is the Lord of all things and he gave us the whole earth with the task to till the soil and enjoy its fruits (Gn 1:26–29; 2:15). Besides, we all benefit from all the inventions and discoveries of past years. They are the patrimony of all mankind. In this sense, we only build on what we inherit: we can hardly be considered original, since none of what we produce or acquire is exclusively the fruits of our labor and talents.

Within this framework exists the right to private property. Important in this respect is the concept of *ownership*. A strict and real right, ownership may be defined as the legal right to dispose of something as one's own. If the title of ownership is based on natural or positive laws, it is called a *legal title*. On the other hand, if the ownership is derived from free agreement, it is called a *contract*.

We shall now discuss each of these two modes of acquiring ownership.

There are four legal titles to property, namely: 1) *occupancy*—taking possession of something unowned like fish, wild animals, minerals, and treasure troves; 2) *finding a lost item*—property that has an owner but one who is unknown (a wallet on a park bench or a mobile phone on a bus seat); 3) *accession*—ownership of the fruit of one's existing property (the piglets belong to the owner of the sow, the trees and crops growing on a property belong to its owner); 4) *prescription*—acquisition through uninterrupted possession after a lapse of time. Each country has its own juridical norms that govern legal titles.[99]

Contract is an agreement between private parties, manifested by a sensible sign, that creates mutual obligations enforceable by law. A contract is a pact over a certain business, a sort of private law that binds the parties to fulfill its terms. The rights and duties arising from a contract are ultimately rooted in natural law, but are protected by human positive law. For a contract to be valid, four elements are required, namely: 1) *suitable object*—it must be capable of being valued at a price (spiritual goods cannot be lawfully sold), it belongs to the contracting party, and it must be morally good and lawful; 2) *qualified persons*—any person who has the use of reason (for example, not a child or one who is deranged or drunk) and is not barred by law can validly enter into a contract; 3) *legitimate consent*—it must be true and internal (not feigned), free and deliberate (desired and chosen), externally manifested (it can be seen and known), and mutual (the parties must agree on the same thing); and 4) *proper form*—civil and church laws often require that contracts follow certain external forms (formalities) for these to be valid, or else the contracts are null and void[100] (for example, the need for earnest money, mortgage approval, and home inspection when buying real estate; the presence of the local Ordinary, pastor or delegated priest or deacon and two witnesses when contracting a canonical marriage).

Unjust Appropriation

Unjust appropriation is when a person unjustly takes as his or her own the property that belongs to another. This can happen in two ways: *theft* or *robbery*. Specifically, *theft* is usurping secretly someone else's possession against his or her reasonable will. Aquinas says that the furtive nature of *theft* is a sign of shame and it somehow removes the scandal. *Robbery*, on the other hand, is taking a property openly, that is, in the presence of its owner and against his or her will, by using violence or sowing fear. Both theft and robbery are acts of injustice, but robbery is more grievous for it involves both a real injustice (as regards the property) and a personal injury (as regards the individual).[101]

The evil of theft consists mainly in the usurpation of another's property against the reasonable will of the owner. Even if it does not violate civil law, any form of stealing is injustice. This includes withholding of goods lent or of objects lost, business fraud, paying unfair wages, cheating, usury, and exploitative overpricing. Theft may be in the form of financial corruption, forgery of checks and invoices, extortion, tax evasion, embezzlement, willful damaging of private or public property, or poor work performance.[102]

Violations against the right to property differ in gravity, but on the whole, the offense is more serious the heavier the damage inflicted. How much harm is caused in turn depends on the reasonable offense, indignation, and disorder caused by the theft.

We call *petty theft* the offense of stealing low-value property, generally less than one thousand dollars in the United States. A typical example is shoplifting, in which the thief is already on the premises; otherwise it could be burglary, which implies breaking into a house or building for the purpose of committing a crime. But petty theft also occurs when a person fails to scan some items in a shopping cart at a self-checkout register, or when he or she switches price tags on items while in a store, or conceals merchandise in his or her purse, or eats and walks out of a restaurant without paying the bill. If we borrow a pair of scissors and fail to return it, not because we forget but in the hope that the owner might not notice, this is stealing. It may not be a grave matter, but it is injustice.

Exceptions are possible in cases of extreme necessity. One may take from another's property what he or she needs, and only these, to relieve hunger, thirst, nakedness, and so forth. It may not sound like good advice, but you may licitly "help yourself" to someone else's goods when you are in serious distress. In the aftermath of a category 5 hurricane, survivors plundered a big shopping mall to grab everything from canned goods and clothes to blankets and flashlights. In extreme cases, the primary need for survival can take precedence over the right to property, although this rarely happens. The Angelic Doctor explains the reason: life is more valuable than material things. The distribution of goods based on civil law does not preclude the fact that human needs must be remedied by means of these very things. Natural law dictates that the superabundance of the haves is due to succor the poverty of the have-nots. But this is justified only when there is present, urgent, and grave necessity under exceptional circumstances,[103] not by caprice, greed, and false needs in normal situations.

Taking something by stealth is not always a theft. If, owing to fear or a moral impediment, someone cannot openly claim what he or she rightfully owns, the person may take it clandestinely. This is called *occult compensation*. It is an extra-legal manner of recovering from loss or damage, by one's private authority, taking the value or equivalent of his or her goods from another who refuses to meet the demands of justice. Moral theologians generally agree that occult compensation is allowed, provided that what is involved is a strict debt (not a matter of convenience), the right violated is certain (well established), there is no other way to recover the debt, and scandal is avoided.[104] When employees are forced to do tasks not included in the contract, compelled to work overtime without pay, or obliged to accept glaringly unjust wages, they can make recourse to occult compensation.

However, there is a risk of abuse in the appreciation of the exact amount due, an arbitrary determination of the strict debt. Thus, it helps to get advice from a person of prudent judgment. Occult compensation may also cause an imbroglio and scandal if it is discovered. For this reason, it must be used only very rarely and as a last recourse.

Occult compensation may have the appearance of theft, but it is really not, since the case involves a debtor who is able, but unwilling, to settle his or her debt and thus restore equality. Jurists and moralists agree to this doctrine, on the grounds that occult compensation is a form of self-protection aimed at setting right what is wrong in the name of justice and equity.[105]

Restitution of Stolen Goods

Restitution, as we have said, is the act of restoring to a former state or position. It is recompense for loss, damage, or injury. When dealing with stolen property, we need to keep in mind four fundamental axioms: 1) the property calls for its owner; 2) the property fructifies (produces) for its owner; 3) the property perishes (expires) for its owner; and 4) no one can enrich himself or herself at the expense of another.

Moreover, the disposition of the person who takes the property has to be considered. Does he or she possess it in *good faith*, believing mistakenly that the property really belongs to him or her based on a seemingly valid title, receipt, inheritance, and so forth? Or does the person lay claim to the property in *bad faith*, holding on to it while perfectly aware that it does not belong to him or her?

If the true owner of the property shows up and reclaims his or her right, the possessor *in good faith* is obliged to return the thing itself, or its equivalent value when the property has been sold or consumed. Besides, he or she is also duty-bound to turn over the natural fruits of the property, such as harvests, earnings, interests, rentals, and so forth, because *the property fructifies for its owner*. However, if the property disappears due to no fault of the possessor, he or she does not have the duty of restitution.[106] If you found a laptop on the backseat of a taxi, got hold of it, and called up and found its owner, but it then got snatched on a street corner before you could return it, the loss is not your fault. You are not obliged to pay for it. In fact, you went out of your way to return the laptop which was in your hands in good faith.

The possessor in *bad faith* has the duty to return the stolen property and make restitution for all the damages that were caused as well as compensate for the forgone income. If the property has been lost, the unjust possessor must pay its equivalent value. He or she may keep only the fruits derived from his or her own labor through the property that served as an instrument. Should the legitimate owner not appear, the possessor in bad faith ought to give it for charitable ends like helping the poor, since *no one can enrich himself or herself at the expense of another*.

The possessor *in doubt* can easily become a possessor in bad faith if he or she neglects the duty to search for the legitimate owner of the property.[107] If the doubt arises after taking hold of the property, a person must try to resolve the doubt. Unable to dispel the doubt, he or she may keep the property, but at the same time must be ready to return it if the rightful owner shows up. Quite different is the case if the possessor is already in doubt when he or she got hold of the property and the doubt persists. There is clear injustice: one is bound to return the property and might have to make a proportional compensation.[108] What would you do if you found a Golden Retriever on the cargo bed of your pickup truck in a parking lot? You just stepped out of a restaurant and here's a lovely pet dog ready to go with you. Will you just drive away with it without first looking for its owner?

Tributary Justice

Persons (physical person or legal entities) are not the only ones who possess rights that need to be respected. The public authority has the natural right to demand from citizens all that is necessary to promote the common good. Part of *legal justice* and *distributive justice*, this implies the duty on the part of subjects to fulfill their roles, including the obligation to pay taxes, exercise the right to vote, and defend their country.[109] Jesus himself paid a shekel tax like everyone else (Mt 17:24–27). Writing to the Romans, St. Paul urged them to be subject to the governing authorities: "Pay all of them their dues, taxes to whom taxes are due, revenue to whom revenue is due, respect to whom respect is due, honor to whom honor is due" (Rom 13:7). Thanks to the amount of tax collected, we have roads, public parks, electric power, postal service, armed forces, health care, public libraries, and so forth. Our money goes to these public services.

Fiscal policies bind in conscience for as long as they are just, and they are just unless there is evidence to the contrary. Restitution is required if a person is guilty of tax evasion. It is not only commutative justice (part to part) that requires restitution, but also legal (part to whole) and distributive (whole to part) justice, since any injustice causes a certain inequality, although the amount to be returned in legal justice is not easy to assess. The *New York Times* reported that the United States is losing up to one trillion dollars in unpaid taxes per year[110] due to misreported income from businesses, farms, sole proprietors, rent and royalties, and capital gains.[111] Such enormous loss can affect budgets for the fire department, civil service, public transport, law enforcement, and so forth. The United States has a big economy, but if this happens in less developed counties, tax gaps easily translate into much poorer public service.

On the other hand, in theory, grossly unjust taxes do not oblige in conscience. This would be the case, for example, if the levies imposed are excessively prohibitive and discriminatory or public funds are clearly used for immoral purposes.[112] Corrupt and despotic governments tend to exact unjust taxes, like the Reich Flight Tax used by Nazi Germany to stem capital flight and practically seize Jewish assets. Paying tax due is a moral obligation, but not when the people's money is used, for example, to finance the state's killing machine.[113] A person may also use every available legal means to reduce his or her taxes. This is not a breach of law, but rather a strict application of its terms and provisions.[114]

As a rule, tax duties morally oblige if they are imposed by the competent authorities, they are based on a just cause, they are proportionate to people's income, the tax revenues are destined for honest ends, and there is transparency in government spending and tax administration.[115] Speaking to fiscal advisers, St. John Paul II reminded them of their duty to protect honest taxpayers from malpractice and help citizens assert their rights, without detriment to their duties to "Render to Caesar the things that are Caesar's" (Mk 12:17).[116]

Hierarchy of Rights

Not all rights have the same importance. Some rights are primary, inherent in every person, like the right to life, freedom of speech, and the truth. These rights do not change. Other rights are secondary. They vary according to our circumstance, responsibility, or state in life. Voters, employees, artists, and students are distinct social groups with different rights that may change across space and time. The trouble is that in today's world primary rights and secondary rights are often confused and swapped. Worse, false rights are invented while real ones are suppressed. You can guess the outcome. "Wrongs" are proclaimed as "rights." Evil deeds become the order of the day.[117]

According to Aquinas, the goods of the human person are threefold: 1) The good of our soul—this is the most important, it cannot be taken away from us; 2) the good of the body—this can be injured by violence and it takes priority over external things; and 3) the good of external things—this can be usurped or unjustly appropriated. Following this logic, murder is worse than adultery and a person's good reputation is more valuable than money, since honor and fame are akin to spiritual goods. That is why slander is generally more serious than theft, though aggravating or extenuating circumstances may change the order.[118]

Procured abortion is a perfect example of a case where there seems to be a conflict between a mother's right to reproductive health and the right of the unborn infant to live. But the conflict is just that: apparent, not real. Other than for very serious reasons (as in a complicated pregnancy that poses a real threat to the mother's life), nothing can justify medical interventions that unintentionally cause the death of the baby (double effect): not emotional well-being, not financial burden, not an abusive relationship, and certainly not fetal abnormality. The moral dilemma of abortion and that of similar issues like euthanasia and divorce is resolved if people appreciate what constitutes authentic human good, the hierarchy of true values, and, hence, the scale of rights in order of importance.

Justice that is not anchored on natural law and ultimately on God stands on shaky ground, as we noted in the first chapter ("Prudence"). Any concept of right and wrong based merely on legal (civil) duty is hollow and feckless. It cannot really put order in our community. The denial of objective, transcendent truth would unleash wild, selfish motives that pit people against each other. Everyone would impose his or her ideas. Arbitrary rule and tyranny would reign.[119] When norms of conduct cannot appeal to any authority higher than the inherently fickle and flawed mind of human legislators, what we have is *legal positivism*, a disease that haunts most justice systems today. Talking about contemporary problems of justice, Dr. Francis Beckwith, an American philosopher, Christian apologist, and professor of church-state studies at Baylor University, shares the same diagnosis in his timely book entitled *Relativism: Feet Firmly Planted in Mid-Air!*[120]

Potential Parts

Since the person is a social animal, we naturally have friends and interact with other people. Every day we communicate, exchange, share, transact, get together, work together, or live together. There is incessant talking, buying, selling, lending, paying, borrowing, returning, agreeing, fulfilling, and so forth. Justice is the virtue that orders agreements, compensations, satisfactions, and restitutions. This cardinal virtue is absolutely essential for social order.

Yet peaceful coexistence cannot be attained solely by justice.[121] Important as it may be, justice is not sufficient to create a humane society. If people deal with each other only in terms of strict duty, if social relations are all done by calculation, then they become cold, rigid, and insensible. A person will continue to be needy, even if no one treats him or her unfairly. Thus, it is not quite right to limit ourselves to rendering what is strictly due. The *just* (broadly understood) person recognizes that one's whole life is a gift and so he or she must do more and give more than the bare minimum. Aquinas aptly said that "[m]ercy without justice is the mother of dissolution; justice without mercy is cruelty."[122]

Justice needs to be complemented by mercy and love for a proper functioning of the political order. This truth is recognized by society occasionally, as when scores of heads of state flew to India in September 1997 for the state funeral of Mother Teresa, held as a fitting tribute for her works of charity and mercy in Calcutta.[123] The diminutive saint showed us that the world needed more than strict justice; she was the face of human compassion and mercy.

In effect, some virtues are similar to justice, but they lack some of its essential properties (*aequalitas*, *debitum*, *alteritas*) if justice is taken in the strict sense.[124] Technically called *annexed virtues* or *potential parts* of justice, they cover those things that we "ought to" do, "must" fulfill, or "should" give, but in a way that we cannot full render or that is not quite as a strict obligation.

Lacking in Strict Equality (*Aequalitas*)

When we owe something to someone but we are not in a position to pay him or her back fully, as much as we want to—when we cannot give anything close to equal what the person has given us through his or her kindness, guidance, example, or leadership—we deal with annexed virtues of justice that fall short of satisfying equality.

1. Religion (religio): *Religion* is the virtue by which we honor God through interior acts (prayer and devotion) and exterior acts (adoration, sacrifice, and vow) of worship. It is fitting to worship God since he is the first cause of all things. Religion is the most important moral virtue, surpassing in perfection even justice itself due to the excellence of its object.[125] Everything in our life is a gift which we ought to acknowledge. So, the first act of religion is thanksgiving. We must also praise and trust God in a spirit of filial dependence on him. Yet our sacrifices, offerings, and rituals for the Divinity are never enough. It is impossible for human beings to give God what he fully deserves.[126]

No matter how holy a person is, he or she will always fall short of what is strictly due to the Lord. A Catholic may regularly go to

Mass, pray the Rosary, and go to confession; a Muslim may faithfully observe Ramadan, give alms, and visit the holy city of Mecca; a Jew may honor the Sabbath, master the Torah, and abstain from pork—but none of them are able to give what the divinity deserves. There is simply no equality between a creature and the Creator. Nevertheless, the Almighty does not ask for what is beyond our capacity. The divine law is not properly called *jus* but *fas*, because God is satisfied if we do what we can. Still, the virtue of justice inclines us to repay and serve God to the best of our ability.[127]

2. Piety (pietas): *Piety* is the virtue that disposes us to honor our parents and our country (after God) as the second principles of our being and government.[128] We may have multiple debts, but the most basic debt on earth is what we owe our parents, our precious life. We would not be here if not for Mom and Dad, who cooperated with God in bringing us into the world. Plus, they fed us, clothed us, sent us to school, taught us the virtues, and so on. Certainly, we did not merit our existence. Now, can we pay back our parents for all their love, toil, and sacrifices for us? They may not be perfect, but just the same, no child is in a position to fully remit his or her filial indebtedness to his or her beloved mother and father. Hence, the *virtue of piety* exceeds the limits of strict justice. As our way of saying thank you, we may shower them with untold gifts, fly them to exotic places, give them the best medical care, or stay by their bedside, yet none of these can pay them enough. We cannot speak of real equivalence here. That is why we must always give due respect and reverence to our parents.

3. Patriotism: Duty to our homeland requires *patriotism*, the virtue by which we pay homage to all our fellow citizens and to all the friends of our country.[129] We cannot totally pay back our country for what it does for us; it is impossible to quantify the benefits we get from public services, be they peace and order, health, education, transportation, or infrastructure. But we practice patriotism each time we pay our taxes, cast electoral votes, fight for our country, or even just stand erect for the national anthem. The civil community as a whole has a certain right to expect loyalty from its citizens, yet this is often undermined by rugged individualism that tends to stress personal rights without the corresponding duties to the common good. President John F. Kennedy's historic words expressed in a nutshell the very idea of patriotism: "Ask not what your country can do for you—ask what you can do for your country."

4. Obedience:[130] We are bound to obey our superiors, a duty based on the natural order and the divine law. The *virtue of obedience* has as its special object either a tacit or explicit command. Every subject of a legitimate authority is morally obliged to obey, whether it refers to parents, public officials, church pastors, school administrators, military officers, or company executives. The duty to obey stems from the order of justice—there is stability in human affairs only if people obey those in charge.

Obedience is not necessarily opposed to freedom. Rooted in the will and the intellect, the virtue of obedience is shown in a person's readiness to embrace the will of his or her superior without losing his or her own identity. A child who obeys his or her parents, a citizen who obeys the state laws, an employee who obeys his or her boss, and anybody who obeys God all become larger than themselves without ceasing to be who they are. An act of obedience is not below human dignity, but well above it.[131]

How much obedience do we owe our superiors? That is hard to measure. When a person obeys externally but rebels internally, we have a case of material obedience shorn of an assent of the will. Anyone who follows the wishes of his or her authority while harboring inner grudges lacks formal obedience, and thus lacks the excellence of the virtue.[132] Obedience implies humility. It is easier to obey if we think that we are not self-sufficient, that we live in a more or less structured world led by authorities, and that our judgment can be mistaken. Obedience rests on the fact that other people have more knowledge, experience, or wisdom than we have or that they are simply vested with power. While we are free and autonomous, there is little nobility in too much self-reliance, in pretending to be totally independent, and in doing our own will.

That said, there is an obvious limit to obedience. We are not expected to follow immoral or unlawful orders. Any command that leads a person to sin or the proximate occasion of sin does not bind. In fact, a person should resist and disobey what he or she is unreasonably asked to do. If students are asked by their teacher to watch lewd shows as part of academic requirements, they ought to disobey and protest. If a military captain is ordered by his or her commander to torture war prisoners or bomb a civilian population, he or she should object. In the famous 1945–1946 Nuremberg trials, top Nazi officials used the "plea of superior orders" in the hope of being acquitted from war crimes, but such defense holds no water for someone with a moral choice.

5. *Reverence:*[133] *Reverence* (technically called *observance*) indicates the respect we show toward persons distinguished for their office or authority. People who possess special dignity deserve respect due to their excellence. Their position implies the exercise of virtues like prudence; they help create a well-ordered communal life. We thus owe them a certain honor and respect. *Reverence* is based on the interdependence of people. No well-ordered society can thrive without leadership and hence, relations of dependence.[134]

Certainly, private individuals benefit from the services of public officials, doctors, teachers, judges, or scientists, creating a sort of debt that cannot be fully acquitted by any form of payment. Nobody really can compensate for a person's authority and ability (moral and intellectual) to rightly administer an office.[135] The labors of countless people in authority are doing us a lot of good in ways beyond measure.

What about unworthy leaders and corrupt public officials? Should we also revere them? Aquinas resolved the dilemma by saying that what we really honor is the dignity of the office and the community as a whole.[136] Incompetent and dishonest officials may have to be removed, but the reverence to the office holds.

Lacking in Strict Obligation (*Debitum*)

Aquinas distinguishes between lawful due (*debitum legale*), which is the object of justice proper, and moral due (*debitum morale*), which concerns the rectitude of virtue. Certain moral due is required to such an extent that, without it, a person cannot preserve moral uprightness (sincerity, gratitude and vengeance) while other moral due is conducive to, but not absolutely required, for virtue (liberality and affability).[137]

1. Sincerity: *Sincerity* is the virtue by which we appear in our life and words as we really are. We are honest if we express what is in our mind, not something else. *Truthfulness* is essential in good relationships; it is the cornerstone of social harmony. Conjugal life is ruined and friendships break apart under the weight of lies. People cannot simply live together if everyone distrusts everyone else, and dishonesty is what breeds distrust. Hence, *truthfulness* is an essential virtue, and it is something due.[138]

But *honesty* is valuable not only for practical reasons. It is a requirement of human dignity. A person knows the other person as another self, an individual of the same nature. He or she thus sees a moral duty to be honest with one's fellow men since, per the Golden Rule, everyone ought to treat others the way he or she wants to be treated—that is, honestly.[139]

Sincerity resembles *justice* insofar as it is directed to another and establishes a certain equality. But they differ by reason of their acts, since justice involves a strict right whereas sincerity implies only a moral right. Hence, insincerity *per se* does not violate a strict right of another, and for this reason it does not require restitution.[140] If someone owes you money, you can rightly demand payment. But if he or she is dishonest with you, you would feel hurt, but there's not much you can do. Still, any form of dishonesty (duplicity, hypocrisy, boasting, simulation, irony, and the like) causes harm to others. The evil of falsehood rests on the motive to deceive others. Lying is *locutio contra mentem* (speaking against one's mind) and this happens when the *external* acts (words, gestures) of a person do not conform to his or her *internal* thoughts. "All dishonesty injures the trustworthiness of the person" and "goes against the dignity of man."[141] A lie establishes a relation of inequality between equals,[142] sowing the seed of discord. Falsehood does real violence to another by affecting his or her ability to know and make correct judgments.[143] The eighth commandment forbids dishonesty.

However, there is a caveat! To be honest does not mean telling all regardless of the circumstances. We do not broadcast intimate things nor reveal secrets—matters we are morally bound to keep from people who do not have the right to know them. Doctors, lawyers, scientists, and government agents must remain silent on confidential information. In fact, it is an injustice to divulge what is meant to be concealed.

Besides these exceptions, everyone should try to be sincere, fostering the habit of telling the truth in the right place, at the right time, and in the right way.[144] "Let what you say be simply 'Yes' or 'No'; anything more than this comes from evil" (Mt 5:37). Honesty is more than just unsullied speech. The way a person behaves is the real test of one's sincerity. This facet of moral life includes a whole range of positive attributes like integrity, loyalty, trustworthiness, fairness, probity, and nobility. An honest person does not cheat, trick, or defraud others, but always acts *bona fide*. Part of sincerity is *fidelity*, the virtue by which we fulfill our promises and remains true to our word. When we make a serious commitment, we are morally obliged to honor it, even if we falter along the way. If *honesty* is rectitude in speech, *fidelity* is rectitude in deeds, inclining us to conform our behavior to what we have pledged to do. Conjugal fidelity and loyalty to our vocation are grave obligations in conscience.

2. *Gratitude*: *Gratitude* is the virtue that inclines us to acknowledge our debt to benefactors who do us favors. Acts of kindness create a sort of obligation on the part of their beneficiaries, the duty to say thank you. Expressing gratitude to a generous friend is giving him or her what a donor naturally expects, even though this is not a strict duty of justice and cannot be enforced. *Gratitude* presupposes a gift freely given, not an obligation that has to be paid. Of course, we may say thank you to the cab driver or bank teller, even if they do nothing more than carry out the job for which they're paid. But this is a matter of courtesy, not strict justice, precisely because *gratitude* falls short of an exact obligation.

Seneca says that we ought to express our gratitude at once, but without feeling obliged to immediately return the favor. Hurrying to pay back, favor for favor, is not a virtue but a constrained repayment. If you receive a gift from a friend and you lose no time in sending him or her a present of equivalent or greater value, you're an unwilling debtor, and an unwilling debtor is ungrateful. Wait for the opportune time to do it, Seneca and Aquinas affirm.[145] It is enough to send a thank you note for now.

3. *Affability*:[146] Social life requires people to behave with propriety and decency. *Affability* or *friendliness* is that annexed virtue of

justice that orders our mutual dealings. We expect people to treat us kindly, so we ought to do the same toward everyone, at the very least acting in a becoming manner. There is a certain natural equity by which a person is obliged to live agreeably with other people.

But this obligation lacks the full aspect of debt; it does not fulfill the requirement of strict justice. No one can hold us legally accountable for not being pleasant with someone, since affability is not a legal but only a moral duty. Still, if we want to be virtuous, let us try to be nice to others in the way we express ourselves and interact with everyone around us. Smile and say hello, listen to someone talking, be sure to say please, don't argue or criticize, hold the door for someone, and so on. Obviously, we are not expected to treat strangers and close friends alike. The degree of familiarity varies, depending on how intimate our relationship is. However, friendliness is a virtue that everyone must observe with everyone else.[147]

4. Liberality:[148] Aristotle says that *liberality* or *generosity* is the virtue that inclines a person to be open-handed (*largitas*), ready to part with things rather than withhold them.[149] Aquinas adds the idea that the word *liberal* connotes the ability to be free (*liberat*) of whatever is in our possession. Letting go of what we keep or own shows an inner disposition of detachment, especially from money and material goods.[150]

Generosity exceeds justice, but the two virtues have points of convergence: they both imply "otherness" and external things. Now, why "ought" we be liberal or generous? What makes liberality a moral virtue? The answer is simple. Liberality shows that a person is not a lover of wealth, that he or she is not greedy but readily uses possession not only for his or her own needs but also to serve others and give glory to God.[151] It is good for people to be generous, but we cannot demand acts of kindness as if this were a strict duty of justice, any more than we can be required to give in excess of our exact obligation.

Generous people bear witness to the fact that humanity needs more than strict justice. They give more and do more than what is required. They are quick to lend a hand, reach out, devote time, go the extra mile, and do anything to make a difference in people's lives. Generous individuals embody the ideal of the selfless and represent everything opposed to the selfish.

5. Equity (Epekia):[152] *Equity* is a less known virtue that loosely means prudent and flexible application of the law. Laws are general norms and broad guidelines. No legislation can foresee all possible events. Situations vary a great deal, such that applying the law strictly in certain cases can do more harm than good. The virtue of equity allows us to set aside the letter of the law and follow the dictates of justice and the common good. Let's say you're driving to the airport at dawn to catch your early morning flight. The traffic light flashes red as you approach a street junction where there's nobody around. Normally, you should wait for the green light, but as things stand, you may proceed with caution for reason of equity.

Equity, of course, is a not a ticket to dispense oneself arbitrarily from the law. It requires prudent discernment so that without being unjust, we avoid at the same time being too rigid and unreasonable. Traditionally, equity asks the question, "What was the original intent of the law?"[153] or, "What was the mind of the legislator in framing the law?" Thus, equity allows a person to preserve the spirit of the law by understanding the motive and circumstances that gave rise to the law in the first place. Equity is a key virtue in interpreting the law and applying it in a particular case, always in view of the common good.

6. Vengeance:[154] *Vengeance* or *vindication* does not sound virtuous at all. But it is actually a good habit of a person who loves justice.[155] God himself will avenge his elect (Lk 18:7). Vengeance is not about striking back at those who hurt us; it is

not an arbitrary revenge that is totally out of proportion. It has nothing to do with the modern idea of vendetta, understood as a blood feud in which the family of a murder victim exacts revenge on the killer and his or her family. Rather vengeance as a virtue is a measured retribution, meting out punishment to the guilty so that the person may amend his or her ways and stop doing more harm to you or others. Vengeance is lawful if it is directed to the good and the circumstances call for it.

We shall see in the next chapter that anger (moderated wrath) is an important element of the virtue of fortitude; it is a proper emotional response that helps us act decisively against evil. Similarly, vengeance is motivated by the desire to restore equality when injustice is committed. It is perfectly allowable to demand due compensation if our property is damaged, our reputation is tarnished, or our dignity is violated. In fact, it is a duty to act in self-defense and re-establish the order of fairness if such is disrupted.

You don't just cross your arms and do nothing if someone snatches your phone or a newspaper runs a slanderous article against you. Surely you won't keep quiet if your salary is withheld for unknown reasons, or if the plumber you hired does a poor job. To act otherwise would be indifference, cowardice, or insensibility, vices that perpetuate injustice. As a means to restore equality, vindication is something due and is essential to maintain good relationships.[156]

Christian Justice

The fourth beatitude states, "Blessed are those who hunger and thirst for righteousness, for they shall be satisfied" (Mt 5:6). Righteousness here is the same as justice, but understood in a wider sense than mere human justice. It is, first of all, a divine quality often mentioned in the Bible. God is righteous and faithful, but he also justifies, saves, and sanctifies. If the just God clothes us in holiness, justice implies a personal relationship with God. The just man or woman is one who obeys God's will. Hence, the primary aspect of hunger and thirst for righteousness is the desire for holiness.[157]

But our relationship with God has a direct bearing on justice and love toward one's neighbor. There is a deep connection between the two. How a we treat other people is the litmus test of our faithfulness to God. Matthew's Gospel states that what we do or fail to do in relation to the least of our brethren (feed the hungry, welcome the stranger, clothe the naked; see Mt 25:41–46), mirrors what we do or omit with respect to Jesus. Christian discipleship is necessarily shown in social justice, which has deep biblical roots in the Triune God who, time and again, shows his love and compassion for the weak, the poor, the vulnerable, and the marginalized.

Since the publication of *Rerum Novarum* (1891) by Leo XIII, the Catholic Church, inspired by the gospel of Christ, has developed a body of social teachings called the social doctrine of the Church in response to modern and contemporary challenges. Critical issues like work, family, wage, property, social inequality, and economic development are analyzed and framed in the light of human dignity and the common good, with a view of building a just and humane world. Over the years the popes have echoed with one voice to the world: there is true peace and authentic progress only when there is justice. Times rapidly change, but the basic principles remain constant, like the primacy of people over things, persons over the state, and work over capital. The origin, the subject, and the purpose of all social institutions is and should be the human person, who naturally needs social life.[158]

Secularist trends and liberal ideologies try to take God out of the picture, but human justice finds its perfect expression in Christian justice. In the theory of justice developed by

Enlightenment philosophers such as Thomas Hobbes and John Locke, human reason alone determines right order in society. But the Church teaches the truth about the person, God, and the world. The order of creation—*ordo rerum*—is the basis of the natural law, which is the participation of rational creatures in the eternal law.[159] The Christian vision of justice holds that the eternal law—the divine wisdom or "how God knows the world to be"—serves as the ultimate foundation and norm of human conduct.[160]

We live in pluralistic world. An attitude of openness fosters healthy social relations. This includes tolerance to opinions and lifestyles that differ from ours, in a spirit of peaceful coexistence. We do not expect everybody to share our own values, but we need not compromise our moral principles and the demands of charity. St. Paul's advice to the Ephesians serves as a useful criterion of conduct: *facientes veritatem in caritate*—"speaking the truth in love" (Eph 4:15).

Justice is shown in deeds, but it implies an attitude of respect and sensitivity toward others. The person next to you is also vulnerable like you. He or she can be hurt. People have dignity and rights, feelings and sensibilities. Everyone has a private space and spheres of freedom that ought to be acknowledged—even if he or she is your dearest friend, your subordinate, or your own spouse. We do well to put ourselves in someone else's shoes and think: How would I feel if I were treated that way? Am I being fair and considerate in what I say and do?

"But seek first his kingdom and his righteousness [justice], and all these things shall be yours as well" (Mt 6:33). Considered as a supernatural virtue, justice is an operative habit insofar as it gives a certain inclination and potentiality for obtaining the supernatural good of life. Therefore, Christian justice has a wider scope than human justice, for it includes things and actions on the level of grace. The terminus of Christian justice is always a person, not just as a human being but as a child of God. Social justice is not so much concerned with what (things) as with who (people) we are called to serve. Rooted in human dignity and the sanctity of life,[161] Christian justice seeks to establish God's kingdom on earth, where Christ would reign in people's minds and hearts.

Charity is the distinctive character of Christian justice. Charity purifies the imperfections of justice applied as a mere natural equity. In any area of life, be it family, work, or social relations, our mutual dealings and the services we render go beyond the strict requirements of justice. Without deeds of charity, social life would be insipid, harsh, and cruel, even if everybody fulfilled his or her strict duties. There is a saying that *summum ius, summa iniuria*, which means, *rigorous justice is rigorous injustice.* Justice is essential, but the social order needs to draw from the deeper powers of spirit which condition the very order of justice.[162]

The whole world was shocked when St. John Paul II was shot in an assassination attempt on May 13, 1981, at St. Peter's Square in Rome. Prayers for his survival were mingled with a loud clamor to pin down his assailant, the Turk Mehmet Ali Agca. The gunman indeed was jailed, but few knew that when the pope was being rushed to Gemelli Hospital, before he lost consciousness, he forgave his aggressor.[163] Ali Agca was incarcerated out of justice, but John Paul II pardoned him out of mercy. That's how far charity can go.

Justice alone is not enough to solve the problems of mankind, says St. Josemaría Escrivá. The dignity of every man and woman, who is a child of God, requires charity which sweetens and deifies everything. Our motive in everything we do should be the love of God, which makes it easier for us to treat our neighbor with love. We have a long road to travel from the demands of strict justice to the abundance of charity.[164]

As the saying goes, *justice* is giving to another what is his or hers, but *charity* is giving to another what is mine.

CHAPTER 3

The Virtue of Fortitude

Eleanor Roosevelt once said, "You gain strength, courage, and confidence by every experience in which you really stop to look fear in the face. You are able to say to yourself, 'I lived through this horror. I can take the next thing that comes along.' *You must do the thing you think you cannot do.*"[1]

These words are a call to fortitude from the longest-serving first lady of the United States. Derived from the Latin root word *fortis* (strong) or *fortitudo* (strength), fortitude is the cardinal moral virtue that makes us firm in difficulties and constant in the pursuit of what is good. Fortitude strengthens our resolve to face trials, conquer fear, resist temptations, and overcome obstacles.[2]

In ancient and medieval Western cultural traditions, fortitude is linked to the notion of a *warrior*. The Greek *Iliad* (eighth century BC) and the Latin *Aeneid* (29–19 BC) are classic epic poems that evoke soldiery duty and heroism. In *La Chanson de Roland* (eleventh century AD), the eponymous hero calls upon his knights to fight bravely in the battle of Roncesvalles, even, in an act of chivalry, refusing to blow his horn to summon reinforcements.

The more familiar English word *courage* has its origin in Latin *cor* (heart), Old French *corage* (heart, seat of emotions), Italian *coraggio*, and Spanish *coraje*. It has come to signify valor, zeal, and inner strength. He or she who is courageous is a person of heart. In the following discussion we shall use the terms fortitude and courage interchangeably.

Strength of Mind

We can deviate from our ultimate end (true happiness, union with God) and be thrown off track, so to speak, in two ways. On the one hand, when base passions get the better of us, we can lose sight of our final goal and cling to pleasurable goods irrationally.[3] These can include a delicious steak, sexual intimacy, a relaxing sauna, a cutting-edge gadget, a leisure trip, and anything else humans tend to like. To moderate our desires, we need basically the cardinal virtue of temperance, the topic of the next chapter.

On the other hand, when we recoil in the face of trials and difficulties, we can also veer away from the path that leads to our ultimate end.[4] If there are pleasurable goods, so also there are arduous goods (from Latin *arduu*: steep, difficult), like a painful medication, a laborious task, a turbulent flight, a complicated pregnancy, a high-risk military operation, and anything that we seek to achieve or protect with difficulty. For these, we need the cardinal virtue of fortitude, which is the subject of this chapter. In sum, temperance operates mainly against inordinate pleasures; fortitude operates mainly against excessive fears.[5]

In a loose sense, the term *fortitude* connotes stability of soul or strength of character, and hence, it may be equated with manliness, akin to Benjamin Franklin's notion of the self-made man and the thirteen-virtue path to moral perfection. Understood as such, fortitude is a general virtue needed for every other moral virtue to act firmly. A good person is one who is interiorly strong. If a person is not courageous, he or she will not overcome the difficulties inherent in the practice of any virtue.[6]

In a strict sense, the virtue of fortitude refers to a person's ability to resist and confront all threats and dangers. According to the Scholastic philosophers, the immediate subject of the virtue of fortitude is the *irascible appetite*[7]—that which deals with the arduous good, or good in the face of an evil to be conquered. Its end is to rein in passions like fear and audacity so as to obtain the good grasped by reason. The truly strong person is not the robust and muscular, but the one who faces the dreadful reasonably. Understood in the strict sense, fortitude is a special virtue.[8]

Our life on earth is a constant struggle. There is always something that gets in the way of our plans, something that poses a threat or makes life difficult. Sometimes it is nothing serious, just a mosquito bite; at other times it can be a formidable challenge, like cancer. Sometimes the contradiction comes from without, like bad weather, a tough job, or false accusations; at other times the problem lies within us, such as cowardice, anger, or sloth. Often the enemy within is harder to beat than the enemy without.

The act of fortitude consists in *fortitudo mentis* and *fortitudo animi* (firmness of the mind) and so the virtue has a rational, sapiential character. In his *Nicomachean Ethics*, Aristotle states that courage strikes a delicate balance between two extremes: cowardice and rashness, fear and boldness.[9] Fortitude keeps our will steadfast in seeking the good despite hardships, but it also controls our will from irrational audacity in our good pursuits.[10] Fortitude arms us with the strength to do what is right, good, true, and just. Amidst the storms of life, the brave person bounces back each time he or she falls, overcomes fatigue and weariness, resists temptation, and fights to protect his or her personal integrity.[11]

Brave and Vulnerable

Ironically, only the vulnerable can be brave. Fortitude implies *vulnerability*, that is, the quality of being subject to a wound (Latin *vulnus*): the ability to be hurt, damaged, attacked, or harmed. Strange as it may sound, no one can be courageous except one who is prone to injury. Injury here means any violation of our dignity, integrity, rights, or inner peace. Whatever assails us, everything negative done against us is injurious.[12] That is why we try to be careful: because we can suffer from anything oppressive and detrimental.

If fortitude presupposes weakness, this virtue is alien to angels because they are pure spirit and, in a way, impregnable. Now imagine that Superman and Spiderman are not just movie and comic characters but real life superheroes who are invincible! They, too, do not have to be brave. Nor can they be, if they are always unscathed. But altogether different is the case of regular persons, because we are fragile. Of all creatures, only humans can be strong (display courage) because we are the only beings on earth liable to suffering. We have something to lose. We are not indestructible. In fortitude, strength and weakness are two sides of the same coin.

In the existential condition of humanity—radically good but fallen, redeemed but weak—life is anything but easy. We experience what we may call a moral tug-of-war, a constant tension between the good and the bad. Our qualities are curbed by natural limitations; our blessings are alloyed with miseries. Deep within every person lurks the principle of opposition that makes him or her inclined to evil, but which he or she can and must overcome. Hence, practicing the human virtues is hard. Our own personal experience attests to this sad reality. Somehow the dark forces always pose a threat to the good of humanity, which ultimately is the possession of the Supreme Good (God).

The passion of fear entails a tendency to flee from the source of threats. Yet this inclination to run away can be resisted and must be resisted if a greater good is at risk that is worth fighting for.[13] Fear becomes a moral defect when we steer clear of what we should not avoid, or shun what we must endure.[14] One way or another we need to conquer our fears. We must slug it out even when the going gets rough.

Being brave does not mean the lack of fear, but the ability to overcome it. It is normal to be afraid; it is human to suffer. We all know how it feels to be scared because we have experienced it. However, while we can all be shaken and held back, some people are more susceptible than others. Faced with the same hardship, the weak-kneed tend to suffer more than the stouthearted, since the latter have greater moral stamina.

Apropos our character differences, the renowned German theologian Romano Guardini states that fortitude begins with self-knowledge and self-acceptance. It is important for us to be aware of our strengths and weaknesses. Courage means the ability to embrace our own existence, with its *chiaroscuro* of lights and shadows, highs and lows, joys and sorrows. What happens to a person is not all the result of his or her own choices. One must learn to face life the way it is configured by his or her sex, health, work, family, or social condition.[15]

What we have just said does not endorse a do-nothing, nonchalant attitude toward our bad habits and defects: anything in our character that needs to be changed must be changed. That said, fortitude is firmly grounded on the reality of our dispositions, temperament, circumstances, and whatever falls to our lot. Desiring something other than what we are, who we are, and where we are meant to be—wishful thinking in other words—is a form of escapism, a lack of courage.

Alcoholics Anonymous uses a prayer that beautifully captures the message we are trying to get across: God, grant me the *serenity to accept* the things I cannot change, the *courage to change* the things I can, and the *wisdom to know* the difference.

Reality of Evil

Fortitude also points to the reality of evil; that is, anything that threatens the good we seek to attain. A courageous person does not only seek the good, but also endures evil for that reason.[16] We need not be daring if nobody or nothing ever stands in our way. Life sails on smoothly. We take everything in stride. But when we meet roadblocks, we need to muster strength. We have to stand up to every challenge. Only with fortitude can we fight our way through. Problems, they say, create opportunities: the opportunity, above all, to be manly. "Brave men and women (as well as cowardly men and women) are not born that way; they become that way through their acts."[17]

Whether evil will actually strike or not, we do not know. Whether we would be able to overcome evil or not, we do not know. Uncertainty is inherent in the virtue of fortitude. There is no guarantee that we will attain our goals. Were it not the case, if a person thought or knew beforehand that everything would turn out just fine in the end, he or she would not make sacrifices. If a student were assured of an A+ regardless of how he or she actually fares in class, he or she would be complacent. But because the student can fail, chances are he or she will work hard. That is the nature of fortitude. What we do matters.[18] Success is not assured. We ought to strive to pursue the good end, doggedly if necessary.

We live in an imperfect world. Sooner or later we shall stumble upon the cross. It takes a good dose of fortitude to face up to life's vicissitudes. How we wish things were easy, that circumstances always worked in our favor! We make the best of plans. But there are always hitches. We hope for a happy turn of events. But we often meet disappointments: career, finance, marriage, health, studies—you name it! They are almost always a mix of laughter and tears, joys and sorrows. We are not sowing seeds of pessimism here, just opening our eyes to the harsh realities of life.

The first enemy of success is dis-*couragement*. People lose confidence and become dispirited when they deal with setbacks as though these were final. Hardly anyone succeeds in just one or two or three attempts. We need to be resilient, overcome self-doubt, think positively, work hard, and keep at it. It is important to be aware of the difficulties, but just so as to be better prepared when they come. Our ability to stay afloat and swim counter-current will enable us to even en-*courage* other people who may be going through tough times. Fortitude can turn the wind of misfortune in one's favor. "When life gives you lemons, make lemonade," as the saying goes.

Suffer for the Good

It is a noble thing to bear any difficulty, but we do not suffer for the heck of it. That would be strange, to say the least. The essence of fortitude is not suffering, but adherence to the moral good, sticking it out all the way to the end. The virtue keeps us intact even if we are beleaguered and hemmed in from all sides. There is a paradox intrinsic to the virtue of fortitude. We suffer injury so that we do not break apart; we face the danger so that we preserve our integrity. "We are afflicted in every way, but not crushed; perplexed, but not driven to despair; persecuted, but not forsaken; struck down, but not destroyed" (2 Cor 4:8–9).

A person loves his or her natural life, not simply because he or she is a person, but because he or she is a *good person* and to the extent that he or she is such. The same applies to everything that preserves us: education, health, love, relationships, success, freedom, happiness, or any other authentic human good. We do not despise what is truly valuable, but may give it up for a greater ideal. Christian martyrs shed their blood not because they abhorred life, but because—forced to make a choice— they loved God (a far higher good) more than their own life. By standing up for their faith, the martyrs conquered the trials, proved heroic, and kept their inviolable dignity.

What makes the martyrs admirable is not their bodily torments but the cause for which they died violently, says St. Augustine. War heroes are decorated with medals of honor not for their battle scars but for their gallant service. Had the firefighters and rescue workers who died in action on 9/11 come out alive, they would still be heroes.[19] For it was not their loss that we praise, but their readiness to suffer in a lofty mission. He is a brave man who is willing to forfeit genuine goods for the sake of something greater.

Consequently, fortitude is not the first and greatest of all the human virtues, even if it subjects man to the most severe trials. For neither difficulty nor effort begets virtue; only the good does.[20] Aquinas affirms that the essence of virtue lies in its ordination to the good rather than the presence of difficulty.[21] "Man achieves . . . dignity when, emancipating himself from all captivity to passion, he pursues his goal in a spontaneous choice of what is good, and procures for himself through effective and skillful action, apt helps to that end."[22]

Wise and Just

If the virtue of fortitude is tenacity in seeking the good, the brave person must know beforehand what is good. Fortitude points to something that precedes it. What conscience tells us to be right and just, we aim at regardless of the sacrifices it entails. Whatever good end is dictated by prudence and justice, fortitude seeks it out through thick and thin. It is for the sake of the good that the courageous person exposes him- or herself to the danger.

Consequently, before a person can be strong, he or she has to be prudent and righteous, he or she needs to have correct judgment and a fair mind. Fortitude simply secures and protects the good and just cause, says the German philosopher Josef Pieper.[23] Recall our discussion on the moral good and moral relativism. Implied in every act of fortitude is the quest for an authentic good, anything that leads to human perfection.

Obviously, we cannot consider as brave the person who is daring in evil pursuits, let alone call him or her wise and just. This is not a superfluous statement. Some people are audacious for the wrong thing and for the wrong reason. Suffer we must, but let it be for a real good or a just cause! A student who has the *nerve* to cheat in a proctored exam is not good. Robbers who *dare* swoop into a tightly secured bank are not good. Pregnant women who muster the *courage* to abort their babies are not good. A writer who *painstakingly* collects data to write a slanderous article is not good. They are all acting cowardly.

Aquinas affirms that fear rests on love. We are afraid only of those things that threaten what we love, whether it is life, family, freedom, honor, or property. If we do not care about any of these, if we do not appreciate the value of these goods, in a sense we have nothing to fear. The greatest love is love of God, so the greatest fear should be losing him, the only one who is absolutely dreadful. "He who fears the Lord will not be timid" (Sir 34:14). One of the seven gifts of the Holy Spirit, the fear of the Lord, is not a servile fear, but a filial one that makes a person aware of God's majesty and afraid of displeasing him, just as a child dreads offending his or her beloved father.

But our love can go awry. We can love the wrong object and in the wrong way. At the root of every disloyalty and idolatry is a misguided heart. Inordinate love is present in every sin, so also inordinate fear is included in every sin. There are false loves and false fears. The greedy person fears losing his or her money and riches. The sensual person fears the loss of pleasure. And so on.[24] Love and fear have to be guided by reason to be truly a virtue.

Life itself is radically good and lovable since it is God's gift. But life is tough; it is not a bed of roses. Courage is required in all aspects of human existence. Fortitude is the courage to be and the courage to live in spite of the obstacles.[25] We all need a certain confidence to face the future. What lies ahead is uncertain, yet we need to have the fortitude to act, build, work, explore, take on responsibilities, and form ties. Living means advancing into the realm of the unknown, which may lie before us like a chaos into which we must venture. A person's strength of character will open a way[26] where he or she can walk through the ups and downs of life.

Acts of Fortitude

We have explained fortitude as the virtue that leads us to face fearful things for the sake of the good. Phrased negatively, courage is the refusal to succumb to evil in the pursuit of what is right. Confronting difficulties involves two aspects: *attack* (*aggredi*) and *endurance* (*sustinere*). They are two acts proper to the virtue of fortitude. But since to withstand evil is harder than to attack it, fortitude is mainly endurance. The very danger a person faces acts to dampen his or her boldness and increase his or her fear. Hence, to remain steadfast in the face of evil is more important than attacking the threats.[27]

We really get to know a person's character not when things go smoothly, but when he or she is tried and tested. The best sailors, they say, do not navigate in calm lakes but rough seas. When we are on the defensive, the only option left for us is to hold our ground and refuse to capitulate. Resistance implies great adherence to the good to the point of sacrificing our life[28] rather than our principles. Fear of trials can bend the human will, but fortitude can bear the difficulties by controlling our fear and repelling evil.[29] *Endurance* speaks of an indomitable spirit, one that latches on to the moral good no matter what happens. Nothing can force a brave person to cave in and compromise, not even that greatest injury and ultimate suffering which is death. We shall go back to this point later on.

To endure pain is not to be passive or apathetic. Externally a person in dire straits may appear inert, but only because of the shackles that bind him or her, a circumstantial cul-de-sac. Yet inwardly a strong person is intact. Viktor Frankl wrote a book, *Man's Search for Meaning*, that has sold millions of copies. It describes the author's horrible experience in a Nazi concentration camp. Starvation, humiliation, fear, and anger crushed the hope of survival of most inmates. Everyone was driven to despair, except those who refused to give up what could not be snatched away—their inner freedom and dignity.[30] No pressure or threat can violate the core of our being if we hang on and rise above the challenge.

But the brave person is ready not only to calmly endure the inevitable evil. He also lunges proactively at any threat or hardship, putting a stop to it whenever possible. Anger is relevant in this respect. It may have a bad image, for it connotes fury, outburst, or indignation, all of which create negative perceptions. But there is such a thing as holy ire, as when Jesus violently cleansed the temple of abusive practices (Jn 2:13–25). If we see a big man kicking and hitting a poor little girl, we should be mad. In effect, reasonable anger is laudable.[31] It facilitates prompt action to stop bad things.[32] As a passion of the sensitive appetite, anger is employed by fortitude. The brave person uses moderated wrath for his or her own act, above all to attack the cause of sorrow or pounce upon evil.[33]

Any effort to remove difficulty is an attack of fortitude. Military operatives who search and defuse a ticking time bomb to avert a disaster need to be daring. It also takes courage for parents to stop the bullying their little kids suffer from other children by confronting the school authorities. If your Amazon order does not arrive, you should complain to their customer service or demand a refund.

Fortitude impels us to tackle the roots of anything injurious to us. It includes the disposition to quash or dispel present dangers, shored up by our self-confidence and the hope of success. There is a real chance of overcoming evil, of getting rid of the hindrance. Otherwise, if we are doomed to fail, it does not make sense to even try. Once again, our efforts and sacrifices matter. It is worthwhile to struggle—*vale la pena*, as they say in Spanish—especially if what is at stake has an infinite value, like the salvation of souls.

Death and Martyrdom

The greatest injury, the ultimate suffering, is death. Every pain inflicted on us, every harm that comes our way mirrors death as the final blow and ultimate violation of life. Fortitude invariably points to death. This virtue is all about willingness to die in battle. Any attitude less than that spoils fortitude and renders it ineffective.[34]

With his characteristic depth and clarity, Aquinas explains that fortitude must bind the will steadfastly to the good in the face of the greatest evils, for only thus can man stand firm against lesser threats. We can only brave other difficulties in life if we are bold enough to meet the worst difficulty or greatest bodily evil, which is death.[35]

That is why fortitude is at its finest in martyrdom, as when a Christian gives the witness of blood. Dying for one's faith is an extraordinary act of fortitude, it is the supreme act of charity. A person loves his or her life more than anything in this world, and hates nothing more than death, especially violent death. Hence, when a person lays down his or her life for the sake of God, he or she is doing the most perfect human act. Jesus said, "Greater love has no man than this, that a man lay down his life for his friends" (Jn 15:13).[36] "Call a person a martyr and you add no further praise," says St. Ambrose. Prove the martyrdom of a person (meaning, he or she died a victim of hatred against the Christian faith or *odium fidei*), and that is enough for the Church to canonize him or her a saint.[37]

History abounds in stories of jaw-dropping acts of bravery by men and women, young and old, who suffered united to Christ's passion and death on the cross. Stephen was stoned to death. Perpetua was pierced to the bones. Sebastian was peppered with arrows. Joan of Arc was burnt at the stake. Maximilian Kolbe was starved to death. They and countless other martyrs prayed for or aided (or both) their executioners to do a "good" job. They overcame the greatest evil—death—in order to attain the greatest good—God. They are the ones referred to in the Gospel when it says, "[T]he kingdom of heaven has suffered violence, and men of violence take it by force" (Mt 11:12).

We can elaborate on one shining example. Thomas More was a literary scholar, eminent lawyer, high-profile statesman, father of four children, and lord chancellor of England. A man of unquestioned probity, he would not acknowledge King Henry VIII's divorce from Catherine of Aragon in order to marry the object of his infatuation, Anne Boleyn (recall the 2003 romantic drama film *The Other Boleyn Girl*). When Pope Clement VII refused to annul the king's marriage to Catherine, affirming the indissolubility of the marital bond, Henry VIII broke ties with Rome. An Act of Succession (requiring people to recognize the children of Henry and Anne as legitimate heirs to the throne) was passed in tandem with the Oath of Supremacy (binding all English subjects to accept Henry as the supreme head of the Church of England). Thomas upheld the dictate of his conscience and refused to take the vow. Prolonged incarceration did not cow him into twisting the truth. Thomas' own wife and several friends tried to persuade him to take the oath and save his life. But he would not budge, undeterred by threats. A kangaroo court found him guilty of treason and condemned him to death by guillotine. Moments before his beheading on July 6, 1535, Thomas declared that he dies as "the king's true servant, but God's first."[38]

A person can be unstinting in his or her quest for true ideals. Our body may tremble and cringe, but no earthly challenge can quash the human spirit, for it is capable of the Infinite (*capax Dei*). Inner freedom is possible even under extreme pressure, because no limited good can determine necessarily the human will. God will not allow us to be tested beyond our strength, and when needed, the Holy Spirit will assist with the infused virtue of fortitude. The Lord's grace is more powerful than human fear.[39]

Daily Heroism

We are not likely to be tested in a crucible as was the fate of Christian martyrs. Dying for one's faith is relatively rare these days, compared to the first centuries of the Church. But we are all called to a different kind of martyrdom—the heroism to fulfill our ordinary tasks and bear the pinpricks of daily life. The strength of fortitude is not destructive but constructive. It is that sort of violence needed to firm up a soft character, tear down walls of comfort, and energize a sluggish attitude.

Some people are quick to roll up their sleeves to rescue earthquake victims, or to put their lives on the line saving people trapped in a house ablaze. These are laudable acts of heroism. But in what is not spectacular, in the humdrum of ordinary life, what kind of stuff are we made of? Do we wake up on time to fix our bed and start a busy day? A firm character is required not only during crunch time but also when we report for work, pay the bills, wash the dishes, or go to Mass. These are the usual occasions to practice the virtue of fortitude, bravery in the little things. Dying to oneself every day can be harder than a momentary feat of courage, since the former implies constant struggle in a protracted battle of attrition.

Difficulties are part of daily life. You may have to put up with your spouse who is a little deaf, or your special child who is headstrong. Perhaps you are not in the mood to cook or clean the toilet, but no one else will do that if you do not step in. Sometimes we are so lazy that we literally have to drag our feet just to answer a phone call or open the door. We feel the heaviness of our bodies such that even the simplest task costs us enormous effort. Yet we just have to keep going and do the daily grind. Fortitude means making many small sacrifices, dying countless little deaths.[40]

We need to develop the habit of conquering sloth, timidity, and fear, which explain our omissions. Fortitude means doing what we must do more than what we like to do. Commitment over preference! A lover of comfort, the self needs to be trained in personal responsibility. One thing at a time, one day after another, until we acquire solid virtues. You might have met a person who does not talk much but who gets things done. Mr. Dependable is there when you need him to fix something, resolve an issue, or finish what someone else has neglected. Perhaps it is time to depend less on him and do the things yourself.

The stories that inspire us most are not those of people who won the jackpot in lotteries and then spent the rest of their lives as couch potatoes. Nor are we really edified by the memoirs of bigwigs whose political and financial clout came by way of inheritance. The truly inspiring stories are about those who worked their way up from humble beginnings, self-made people who succeeded by dint of sacrifices.

Fortitude ought to be practiced according to our state in life and personal circumstances. Parents must be strong for their children, whether it is about changing diapers, putting bread on the table, or sending their kids to school. People with specific commitments to God must persevere and remain faithful to their vocation, overcoming doubts and temptations. Emergency room doctors must be decisive and composed in assessing and treating patients regardless of their illness and injury. There is hardly any situation in life where courage is dispensable.

The practice of virtues is anything but easy, for it requires constancy and perseverance. We do not always get it right. So we need to start over and over again. With effort we can develop good habits, even as we try to root out certain defects. It helps to break down big goals into many little objectives and get used to fulfilling our resolutions. We grow as a person by seeking excellence in everything we do. Fortitude leads us to be steady and rise above impulses, whims, and instincts. We may not be in full control of what occurs around us, but we can certainly direct our own steps and put order in our life. Fortitude is the key to human maturity.

St. Josemaría Escrivá, the "Saint of the Ordinary," tells us that fortitude is a certain strength of the will to overcome the fear of effort and of difficulties.

> The person with fortitude is one who perseveres in doing what his conscience tells him he ought to do. . . . The strong man will at times suffer, but he stands firm; he may be driven to tears, but he will brush them aside. When difficulties come thick and fast, he does not bend before them.[41]

When ordinary virtues fail to overcome difficulties, the heroic virtues come to the rescue. Fortitude, in particular, adds heroism in the exercise of any virtue. Over centuries the Catholic Church has enrolled in the roster of saints countless men and women who were not strictly martyrs but who lived their ordinary lives with heroic virtues. The process of canonization starts with an inquiry into how a candidate for sainthood practiced heroism in daily life.

Contrary Vices

Passions must be guided by right reason so that we act in a balanced way and do not get carried away. Otherwise, we would avoid things that we ought to pursue or seek after those that we are supposed to steer clear of. The various difficulties that we encounter in life need to be handled well. If the emotions elicited by the trials are not moderated by fortitude and its parts, we fall into one or more vices against courage.

1. Cowardice

Cowardice or *timidity* is disordered fear of temporal ills. It is a defect of character that consists in refusing to face risks or dangers when we are obliged to do so. Society despises and stigmatizes cowardice. In England during the First World War, women gave white feathers as a symbol of cowardice to men not in uniform to shame them publicly into taking up arms. Of course, not all able-bodied men in civilian garb were afraid to fight, and the white feather campaign had in fact a big backlash, but generally cowardice of soldiers in combat is a crime. Just as bravery is a mark of nobility, cowardice is scorned as a trait of the fainthearted.

The world is not always at war, but each of us has his own personal battles. Regardless of life's circumstances, we are bound to face obstacles. So if a person does not have the heart—is not courageous enough—to suffer pain or bear the contradictions, he or she will, in a way, flee from life itself. Men and women who are scared of family responsibilities will not get married. A person with hemophobia (fear of blood) avoids injections and hospitals. Boxers who dread losing a bout would not fight tough opponents. Students with stage fright would shun recitation in front of the class. Anyone who is afraid of the consequences of telling the truth would tell a lie. Individuals who are scared of rubbing others the wrong way would close themselves off and stay aloof. Nobody goes far in life until the person conquers his or her own fears. Shakespeare wrote, "Cowards die many times before their deaths; / The valiant never taste of death but once."[42]

Sometimes our fears have a real basis. But they can also be self-made fears born of an imaginary threat, the fear of the unknown. A host of "what ifs" or conditionals can paralyze us. What if something bad happens? What if I fail? What if my plans fall through? There are people who dramatize events and conjure up bleak scenarios, so that they are tied down not by real problems but by inner fears. Moreover, our generation often resorts to antidepressants and sedatives as a quick-fix, stopgap approach to handle pressures, fears, and anxieties. Treatment and therapies do help and may even be necessary, but there is really nothing like the strength of fortitude, accompanied by prayer.

People who lack fortitude and do nothing about it have deep-seated insecurities. There is self-dissatisfaction over their mean spirit and small stature. The slightest challenge unsettles them, and since peace is a consequence of war (*pax in bello*), their refusal to fight and endure trials deprives them of inner tranquility. The coward is emotionally out of kilter, imprisoned by timidity. Fears keep him or her away from the course of action pointed to by reason.[43] Faced with a tough challenge, we need to think things over, but at some point we just have to launch into it. The future is uncertain and every plan carries some risks, but only if we cross the Rubicon[44] can we ever succeed in anything worthwhile. As the saying goes, *a cat in gloves catches no mice.* Failure is what we get from overcaution and pussyfooting.

There is also cowardice in someone who chooses lesser goods over higher ones. Fortitude is the capacity to bear difficulties for the sake of a higher good over a lesser one, let alone something that is not good at all. If your right eye or right hand causes you to sin, tear it out or cut it off, for it is better to be maimed and yet saved, than be physically intact and yet damned (Mt 5:29–30). Spiritual evils are to be feared more than bodily pains because the body is destructible, while the spirit is not.[45] A brave person would fear committing a lustful act more than suffering ankle sprain. Yet bodily harms are more to be feared than external threats. Thus, developing an ulcer is worse than losing a mobile phone. Health is important, and so is having a phone, but not in the same degree. Do we often lose sleep to watch late-night TV shows? That is not fortitude, but disorder. Do we work double time to finance a vice? That is not fortitude either, but sensuality. There is a hierarchy of values that a strong person ought to respect and protect.

The hierarchy of goods is important especially among people in authority whose decisions have social impact. Out of prudence a bishop may refrain from denouncing rampant drug trafficking in his diocese to avoid retaliations. But his silence can also be a sign of cowardice and a cause of scandal among the faithful. In the same vein, a politician who panders to the unjust demands of a lobby group just to avoid the political cost of losing votes is not a strong leader but an opportunistic coward. He or she sacrifices the common good for his or she vested interest.

Another manifestation of cowardice is false human respect that stems from a mistaken notion of charity. When we fail to correct a friend who is in grave error on the pretext that he or she might feel hurt or slighted, we sin by culpable omission. We shrink in fear from what we must do. Conscience tells us to do something, but false humility holds us back. It certainly requires fortitude to admonish someone, just as it is convenient to keep silent and spare oneself the hassle of giving a fraternal correction. People sometimes regret not having spoken early enough, clearly enough, and forcefully enough.

2. Fearlessness

To be strong is praiseworthy, but there are times when fear is reasonable. We are not courageous if we endure the things we ought not to; we are just *fearless* or *impassible*. This is not a virtue, but a vice against fortitude. Courage is braving the dreadful in the right way, at the right moment, and for the right reason.[46] Fortitude is not the absence of fear, but the ability to handle fear reasonably.

In the face of evil, we humans instinctively react by way of "fight or flight." The absence of the natural fear may be of psychological origin, but it can also be a moral defect, as when a person fails to appreciate the value of the goods[47] at stake (for example, property, health, reputation, or life). One who does not treasure something is not afraid to lose it.

Moreover, there is a real fortitude and an apparent one. People may carry out difficult or risky tasks blithely because of ignorance. They launch into a dangerous enterprise unaware of its pitfalls and perils. Walking on a field dotted with landmines is not courage if the fellow is oblivious of the explosives. Similarly, a person may find something easy just because he or she is so adept at it, whereas the same activity can be very challenging for others. Taking up differential or integral calculus can be an uphill battle for a student poor at math, but not so for a math

wizard. Public speaking may be a handicap for a farmer, but
certainly not for a broadcast journalist. Finally, it is not courage to do anything out of impulse or passion, no matter how
hard it may be, as when we leap over a high fence on an adren-
aline rush while being chased by German shepherds. None of
the above examples are acts of fortitude since no moderation
of fear is involved. The virtue of fortitude presupposes fear felt
and conquered.

3. Recklessness

If the coward lacks courage, the reckless person has, in a way,
a bit too much of it. *Recklessness* or *temerity* or *rashness* is the
vice that consists in risking danger without proportionate
cause. By misjudging the reality of hazards, the reckless person throws him- or herself into a precarious situation. He or
she acts with rash daring and presumptuous boldness. Anyone
who swims on an icy lake just to set a Guinness world record
is not brave but foolhardy. So, too, are we if we leave our gap-
ing wound untreated, claiming that we never get infected. We
are presumptuous. We also call reckless the fellow who drives
his or her vehicle in wanton disregard for the safety of people
and property.

Recklessness looks like courage because the person is bent
to pursue something in spite of the dangers. But the trouble is
that he or she fails to estimate the real threats which fortitude
recognizes. The brave person is well aware of the risks and is
not exempt from sensations of fear. Courage, not false opti-
mism, is what drives us to face the challenge. The vice of recklessness is rooted in immoderate audacity or in unregulated
passion of daring.[48]

In a sense, we would expect a normal person to be afraid
of evil, or any threat. Being brave and scared at the same time

is possible. And if the person is strong, he or she would likely conquer his or her fear. What is odd is when a person ignores the grave difficulties or acts as if he or she had superpowers. Some people mistake rashness for courage. Just because a person risks any danger does not mean he or she is brave. Fortitude is not about facing arbitrary threats, but self-sacrifice in keeping with reason, that is, in accord with the true nature and value of the goods at stake.[49] Thus, when a group of storm chasers I know bravely basked in the raw power of a tornado to record the severe weather phenomenon, their daredevil hobby (not serious research) was not exactly an act of fortitude, but of plain recklessness.

Temerity can also be the manifestation of a perverted love, an inversion of the natural order, as when one loses the will to live or to do anything good in life. Indifference and despair can make a person insensitive to real threats, like those who jump off the Golden Gate Bridge or Eiffel Tower in an act of despair. Brave people do not suffer delusions of invincibility. They follow the natural order of things.[50] They know that they can be hurt and would avoid anything harmful if doing so stands to reason.

Annexed Virtues and Contrary Vices

What fortitude does amidst the greatest hardships (even danger of death), other virtues take up in the face of minor difficulties. Magnanimity, magnificence, patience, and perseverance are considered *integral parts* of fortitude (that is, essential features) needed when a person faces a matter of life and death. But the same four *integral parts* become *potential parts* of fortitude (independent but annexed to it) when it comes to non-life-threatening difficulties. Magnanimity and magnificence concern *aggredi* (attack), while patience and perseverance pertain to *sustineri* (endurance).[51] Below are the four annexed virtues of fortitude and their contrary defects.

1. Magnanimity

Magnanimity (from *magnus animus*, "great soul"). It is the virtue that inclines us to carry out great deeds, to outdo ourselves in a way, to go far in everything good in spite of the difficulties involved. A magnanimous person thinks big and dreams big and stretches forth his or her mind to great honors with a healthy sense of self-confidence. But a magnanimous person is not after financial success, Olympic gold, academic titles, or Hollywood fame but instead sets his or her eyes on moral excellence. A magnanimous person uses his or her wealth, repute, and God-given talents to serve and accomplish deeds of virtue. This person is not a crowd pleaser or a social climber. Neither fearing criticism nor seeking praise, the magnanimous person speaks his or her mind if needed. Among the great, he or she is great; among the lowly, he or she is unassuming. Generosity, beneficence, and gratitude are among this person's notable qualities. Every virtue enhances human character, but magnanimity adds a certain glow and raises it even more to a higher stature. That is why a magnanimous person is said to be high-minded, yet nevertheless remains humble.[52]

You have probably met people who are so kind and generous to everyone. They give gifts or offer sincere help without expecting anything in return. They go the extra mile to serve family and friends. When offended, they are quick to forgive, rising above anger and petty resentments. They reach out to offer peace even if they are not at fault. Unlike most people, they go beyond their minimum obligations in order to give more and do more. Magnanimous individuals possess noble character and lofty spirit. They give bold testimony to others about how life ought to be lived.

a. Pusillanimity

If the magnanimous person tends to great things, the *pusillan-imous* (from *pusillus animus*, small soul) does the opposite: he or she shrinks. The vice of pusillanimity inclines us to shy away from works that we deem too much for our strength, when in fact they are not. It is a character defect rooted in a person's undervaluation of his or her own qualities and the fear of failure to meet expectations.[53] In common parlance, we call a person *timid* or *fainthearted* if he or she lacks self-confidence equal to his or her talents and does not have the drive to accomplish what he or she must and can. Hence, a wonderful opportunity is lost. Worse, the fainthearted person often drags down the road of discouragement other people who have the potential to collaborate in the great good left undone.[54]

In *The Wizard of Oz*, an American children's fantasy novel by L. Frank Baum (with movie and Broadway musical versions), there is a character called the Cowardly Lion who is in fact brave, like all lions are supposed to be, but whose fear makes him think he is inadequate. He doubts himself, retreats before a velvet fog, and walks on his hind legs. Albeit fictional, the Cowardly Lion embodies a pusillanimous spirit that fortitude must overcome.

b. Presumption

Presumption is a vice against magnanimity by excess. It is rooted in pride and consists in overestimation of one's capacities. If pusillanimity is lack of self-confidence, presumption is overconfidence. It implies a certain blindness to one's real limitations, and so the presumptuous person tends to seek what is above his or her power. He or she longs for honor and recognition beyond what he or she truly deserves. The most profitable business in the world, they say, is to buy people for what they are worth and sell them for what they think they are worth. One can imagine the large margin of profit.

c. Vainglory

Aquinas says that seeking glory in itself is not wrong, citing Matthew 5:16: "Let your light so shine before men." What is wrong is the desire for empty glory or *vainglory*. A vice against magnanimity by excess, vainglory consists in exalting what is unworthy, seeking honor from someone with little merit ("It is better for a man to hear the rebuke of the wise than to hear the song of fools," Ecclesiastes 7:5), or desiring praise without reference to God.[55]

We can detect signs of vainglory in people who are boastful in words, those who show off their possessions, those who stubbornly hold on to their opinions, and those who cannot obey rightful commands. They are also given to discord, hypocrisy, arrogance, and love of novelties. Inability to appear inferior to others is the common thread of all these manifestations of vainglory. Aquinas calls these defects "daughters of vainglory."[56]

d. Ambition

Taken in a positive sense, *ambition* is good. It is perfectly alright to nurture noble dreams and aspirations. Our high school yearbook probably still keeps a record of how we saw ourselves ten, twenty, or thirty years hence. Never mind if what we fancied to become then did not materialize. The point is we should aim high in life. But the word *ambition* may also have a negative connotation, as when it refers to a worldly and superficial quest for honor. An ambitious person uses his or her gifts and abilities for selfish ends. He or she seeks honor for its own sake, not for noble motives. In a nutshell, ambition is the disordered love of honor.[57]

2. Magnificence

When we have a big heart, we have a broad horizon and stretch forth to that which is larger than self (self-interest, personal comfort, narrow concern). This desire to go beyond one's own little world is shown in deeds of service, including the use of wealth if we happen to be rich. *Magnificence* (*magna facere*, to make great things) or *munificence* is the virtue that inclines us to undertake great and costly works in spite of the effort, sacrifices, and expenses this entails.[58]

A person goes beyond him- or herself when he or she serves God and society. It is OK that we take care of ourselves, but we do not become great if all we care about is our work, rest, savings, property, hobbies, plans, and so on. Great men and women leave a lasting legacy for others. Magnificent things obviously need resources. Hence, only wealthy individuals can carry out magnificent or huge projects[59] like building a shrine, monument, hospital, sports complex, orphanage, or museum. Inherent in the virtue of magnificence is the disposition to do good to others, to carry out enormous tasks, and to use riches in the proper way. Excessive love of money, for instance, would be a spur for the wealthy to lavish money on themselves and a disincentive for them to spend for altruistic ends.

Can the poor be magnificent? Inwardly, they can. By choice and intention, a person without means can be magnanimous. But Aquinas affirms that goods of fortune are requisite as instruments to realize outwardly the virtue of magnificence. Only the affluent can accomplish this. Even a generous person cannot perforce do magnificent tasks. He may be kind and liberal in giving gifts and helping others *within his means*, but magnificence presupposes big financial outlays, according to the Angelic Doctor. Magnificence goes beyond liberality.[60] The virtue produces great works in quantity, value, and dignity. It concerns grand actions, courage, excellence, honor, generosity, and splendor for noble ends.

Since God is the greatest good, the most laudable project is anything meant to honor God and divine worship, anything that fosters holiness. St. Peter's Basilica in Rome is the fruit of a collective effort and is one perfect example of a work of magnificence. A quintessence of Renaissance architecture, its elaborate façade, dome, columns, apses, portals, nave, porticoes, statues, inscriptions, and baldachin speak for themselves. This great Christian temple is huge even by modern standards.

a. Prodigality

Wastefulness or *prodigality* is giving too much, spending beyond one's means, while not earning sufficiently or getting enough resources. This is the vice of people whose lifestyle (even if they are benefactors) does not match their economic status. Financial outlay that exceeds the value of the project is a waste.[61] The disorder of prodigality lies in the disproportion of the expenditures vis-à-vis both a person's capacity and what the enterprise requires.[62]

b. Meanness

Meanness is the defect of those who spend less than the worth of their work.[63] It is not uncommon to find people who are affluent but reluctant to share or use their resources for the benefit of others. They have great wealth, but a tiny heart. Or if they begin to support a big venture, they back out midway through, leaving unfinished what they have started. Rich people may be aware of the great good they can do and their tremendous potential to finance large-scale projects for the good of society, but if they are not magnanimous, if they are stingy, they will just pinch pennies.[64] The magnanimous person is a philanthropist who is anything but niggardly.

3. Patience

The Cambridge dictionary defines *patience* as "the ability to wait, or to continue doing something despite difficulties, or to suffer without complaining or becoming annoyed."[65] Derived from the Latin verb *pati* (to suffer), patience is a potential part of the virtue of fortitude. The virtue of patience enables us to bear the present contradictions without giving in to sorrow, especially if these are caused by other people. Sadness or sorrow pulls us down unless we do something about it. By carrying the burden and suffering the hurt, the patient person acts in a praiseworthy manner.[66] The more patient one is, the more calm and equanimous he or she is amidst trials, which is to say that the virtue admits of degrees. One can bear the trials with resignation, without grumbles, or even with joy.

Otherwise known as forbearance, patience is an important virtue in daily life. Things do not always turn out as planned. Sometimes, everything that can go wrong goes wrong. But we do not lose our composure if we are patient. Thanks to this virtue, we learn to be detached from our own ideas, comfort, preference—in other words, ego. Patience is the key to better stress management and healthy relations with other people. We listen to what others have to say. We slow down and pay attention to details. Tempers are held in check. Petty things do not ruin our day. We can laugh at our own mistakes and forgive ourselves. Decisions are not rushed and issues are calmly handled. Patience is thus a sign of self-dominion, and its hallmark is inner peace.

Sometimes the best course of action is just to wait. The following lines from a motivational book may sound clichéd, but there is wisdom in its idea to let things take their natural course. "A baby needs nine months in his mother's womb and being born prematurely brings on complications. You can't pull out an emerging butterfly from its cocoon or else you'll cripple its wings for life. Hurrying a fruit to ripen doesn't make it as sweet as when it does so on its own."[67] Waiting may be hard to do, but it is often the best way to get a blessing. This is true not only in natural processes, but also in most of the things we do every day.

Related to patience is *longanimity,* the virtue that moderates hope by bearing upon a good that is a long way off. Sometimes it takes time to obtain the good we hope to achieve. Prolonged delays do not cause us pain if we have a longanimous spirit.[68]

a. Impatience

Opposed to patience is, logically, *impatience,* which is the defect of one who easily yields to obstacles and reacts by way of complaint and anger. An impulse of the passion of sorrow, impatience stems from the desire to be in control of everything or do things "my way," and since this does not always happen, we get upset and irritated. The inability to wait, tolerate opposition, or handle negative turns of events agitates the person who lacks patience. He loses composure owing to a disordered sadness triggered by contradictions. What a patient man bears with fortitude, the impatient suffers with vexation.

We all have our fair share of impatience. But some tend to overreact, getting easily annoyed by heavy traffic, a long queue at a ticket booth, or a slow wi-fi connection. Our digital age fosters a culture of instant gratification that makes people unable to wait and cope with delays. At times we meet heavier crosses like a grave illness, huge debt, job loss, or the burden of attending to an elderly person. Whatever weighs on us, it pays to tame the impulse of distress and practice the virtue of patience.

b. Insensibility

Being patient is not the same as being impassive. If impatience is overreaction to difficulty, *insensibility* is too much patience, so to speak. The insensible person does not allow him- or herself to be moved by sorrow when he or she should. This person endures pain when he or she should not, thus allowing the unnecessary hardship to perpetuate. We are meek in a wrong way if we do not try to remedy our problems; we tolerate unjust situations. Certainly there is nothing praiseworthy about patiently bearing harm against others, against the common good, and against God's honor. What appears like forbearance is actually a façade of a cowardly spirit.[69] Insensibility implies dullness of the mind and goes against right reason.

It is not wrong to correct what troubles us. To remain impassive before an injustice is not patience, but spinelessness. It is part of fortitude to call the attention of your neighbor if he or she keeps throwing garbage onto your property, or to talk to your professor if he or she gives you a grade incongruent with your real class performance. Allowing these to go unchecked is not patience but insensibility.

4. Perseverance

Perseverance is yet another potential part of the virtue of fortitude. It is basically patience but extended in time, prolonged until the end of trial. Perseverance disposes us to persist in doing what is good despite weariness, tedium, or fatigue.

Sometimes we embark on an undertaking and toil for a time, but at some point we give up. We struggle, yet not all the way. For example, we tend to get excited with anything novel: new work, new colleagues, a new project, a new schedule, and so forth. There is thrill, expectation, and motivation. But soon the monotony of repetition takes its toll. We begin to slow down little by little. Hard work saps our energy. Our drive to excel fizzles out. Boredom sets in. Competing interests fill our mind. We tend to lose focus, make little compromises, and allow idle moments. We have duties to fulfill and yet we do not seem to be capable doing even the simplest things. The culprit is not necessarily poor health, but the lack of moral disposition to hang in there and carry on.

Perseverance helps us to finish what we have started. Of course, in what refers to humanity's final end (salvation), we need to persevere *usque ad mortem* (until death). But we also need to persevere in relatively short-term goals like getting a college degree, completing dental treatments, or even just cleaning the garage. Someone who has resolved to pray regularly or follow a plan of life also needs to persevere in his or her good resolutions. If we slack off in what we have set out to do, failing to accomplish our task, we are guilty of lack of perseverance.[70] St. Josemaría Escrivá said that people like to celebrate the groundbreaking or laying of the first stone of an edifice. "I like to bless the last stone," he said, referring to the importance of a work well finished.[71]

Perseverance is akin to the virtue of constancy in that both virtues imply steadfastness. But they differ in one important point. A person is *constant* if standing firm against external hardships: he or she is *persevering* if steady despite inner resistance that stems from weariness or fatigue. In other words, constancy is facing outside pressures; perseverance is overcoming our own softness.[72]

The Spanish mystic St. Teresa of Ávila (1515–1582), founder of the Discalced Carmelites, beautifully wrote in her *Way of Perfection* about the importance of perseverance. She encouraged her religious sisters not to give up even if they were exhausted, even if they could not go on, even if they burst, even if they died.[73]

a. Feebleness

Opposed to the virtue of perseverance is *feebleness* or *irresoluteness*. As the name suggests, it is the defect of people who fail to sustain the effort required to achieve their goals. Anything good in this world has a price; anything worthwhile requires sacrifice. Only the persistent get things done eventually. The effeminate and wimpy just quit for no other reason than weakness of character. There are those who start a weight-loss program but give it up soon after. Others resolve to be punctual at work but then slacken after an initial fervor. Irresoluteness is often the root cause of one's inability to rise to any serious challenge in life.

b. Pertinacity

There is a false perseverance that characterizes a person who is obstinate and stubborn. This person does not seem to fail at all in whatever he or she is intent on achieving. It looks like a virtue but is really not, due to lack of prudence. We fail in the pursuit of a true good when we seek to "be right" and "appear undefeated" even if holding on to our plans no longer makes sense. *Pertinacity* is a vice of the self-serving, not a virtue of the strong. If you plan with friends to scale a mountain peak but a major landslide weakens its slopes before your trek, it might seem brave to go on with the adventure, but it can also be sheer pertinacity.

Also known as obstinacy, stubbornness is an excess of perseverance rooted in the disordered love for something a person craves, or the refusal to bear the pain of losing something he or she should let go of.[74] It is the defect of the headstrong and opinionated person who insists on his or her own way and humiliates his or her opponents. If the feeble person falls short of perseverance, the obstinate one shows an excess of it. He or she desires the proximate end a bit too much, losing sight of the bigger picture. Cicero said that what superstition is to religion, pertinacity is to perseverance.[75]

Work and Industry

Work is one important aspect of human life where the virtue of fortitude is essential. We have the natural vocation to labor, to "be fruitful" and "fill the earth and subdue it" (Gn 1:28). In a sense, you and I were born in order to labor—*ut operaretur*, to cultivate and till the soil (see Gn 2:15), just as the birds are born in order to fly (see Jb 5:7). St. Josemaría, champion of the hidden value of ordinary life, said that "work is a magnificent reality . . . an inexorable law which, one way or another, binds everyone."[76]

In the previous sections we said that our daily tasks require fortitude, but the notion of work itself deserves a closer look. Whether we enjoy what we are doing or not, work requires effort and exertion. Whether it is intellectual or manual work, we experience fatigue, tiredness, and exhaustion. Hence, fortitude and its annexed virtues are necessary in the fulfillment of our obligations. Where else do we usually need to be patient, constant, tough, and persevering if not in our workplace? The doctor, professor, lawyer, and banker, as well as the farmer, housewife, bartender, caregiver, and truck driver need to be strong. Day in and day out, from dawn to dusk, we put our hands to the plow, even though it is taxing, onerous, and arduous.

Motivational speakers and self-help books may call it "drive for excellence," "habits of a good leader," or "secret to success," but the core of a good work ethic is character maturity, and by and large it means fortitude. We may strive to perform well in view of a job promotion, a pay hike, or professional prestige. But there is a deeper reason why we need to give our best. Work is a requirement of human dignity. It adds to our personal worth. Virtues make us a better person and work is a school of virtues: patience, obedience, loyalty, order, diligence, honesty, dedication, integrity, generosity, and fortitude.

In his landmark encyclical *Laborem Exercens*, St. John Paul II said that work is not just an activity but an integral part of our earthly existence. This is the basis of the dignity of work. Created in the *image and likeness* of God (see Gn 1:26–27), we are the subject of work and through it attain self-realization. Even if we must eat bread by the sweat of our brow (see Gn 3:19), in spite of all our toils work is good for us, because it helps us achieve human fulfillment.[77]

Work is uplifting if a person responds to the call of duty with industriousness. *Industriousness* or *industry* is the quality of being hardworking and diligent. Also called *laboriousness*, the virtue implies an earnest effort to carry out what needs doing. It involves application, firmness of purpose, and determination in our undertaking. *Diligence* (from the verb *diligo*), on the other hand, adds the nuance of love, choosing to care and give attention, being assiduous and steady in effort.[78] In classical ethics the virtue of diligence is illustrated with a woman holding a whip and spurs, signifying the drive to steadfastly move forward with one's means. All these presuppose the virtue of fortitude.

Work also transcends the sphere of individuals. It is bound up with our duty to contribute to the common good, to build up society.[79] This is the heart of social responsibility. We labor to help make this world a better place to live. "Be fruitful and multiply, and fill the earth and subdue it" (Gn 1:28). Placed at our disposal is the vast deposit of natural resources of Mother Earth. Using brains and brawn, we must provide for our needs, support our family, and help in the cause of social progress.

The enemies we need to conquer are sloth, indolence, and laziness—in a word, lack of fortitude. Aquinas defines sloth as an oppressive sorrow that so weighs upon a person's mind that he or she wants to do nothing. One of the capital sins, sloth is a certain weariness that draws a person away from good deeds.[80] St. Paul warned Christians of work-shy people and social parasites who exploit fraternal spirit for their daily sustenance. The Apostle of the Gentiles pulled no punches, if only to teach them a lesson: "If any one will not work, let him not eat" (2 Thes 3:10). God gave us talents so that we may put them to good use and bear fruit. That means work.

Despite the fatigue and weariness it brings, work—honest work—ennobles every person. In a sense, it frees our spirit from the domination of matter and of the body. Each task accomplished, every product of our hands, is linked up with the joy of victory over material things and over ourselves. The working person reaches, as it were, the border between heaven and earth. If done with love, our daily work has a redeeming value. Human labor is a path to holiness, a means of union with God. Somehow the world is unfinished and the Creator calls us to cooperate in his creative and salvific mission.[81] Jesus himself was a carpenter (Mk 6:3) who worked with his human hands and who thus taught us the infinite value of work.

Christian Fortitude

Man is endowed with natural strength to brave the difficulties in life. In a way the human person is hardwired to fight in order preserve his or her integrity. We are capable of great sacrifices in the pursuit of high ideals. The mind can be firm and unyielding for the sake of the good.[82]

Paradoxically, the human person is fragile. In our creaturely status, we wrestle with inherent limitations; in our fallen nature, we are prone to fail. Wounded by original sin, we find ourselves assailed by the so-called enemies of the soul and the triple concupiscence of the devil (the father of lies), the world (empty values), and the flesh (disordered passions). We are easily overwhelmed by obstacles from within us and from without. Life's burdens can surpass our ordinary power such that we need special help if only to remain steadfast. Left on our own, we can give up the fight and succumb to evil, especially if we are pushed to our limit.

Thanks to the Holy Spirit, we receive the gift of fortitude that infuses confidence into our soul, quells any fear, delivers us from dangers, and leads us to eternal life, which is the end of all good deeds.[83] This *supernatural virtue of fortitude* acts not simply with the light of natural reason, but is illumined by faith. *Christian fortitude* is bestowed by divine grace, aids our human weakness, elevates natural fortitude, and is nourished by the hope of final victory. The infused virtue of fortitude is associated with the gift of the Holy Spirit, which has an identical name and which makes us more docile to the promptings of God. Without this supernatural aid, we risk falling into a voluntarism that rests merely on human willpower.

The newfound confidence of a Christian depends not on his or her own capacity to survive, but on God's omnipotence[84] and the fact that nothing but sin can separate him from the Almighty. St. Paul expressed this certainty in his Letter to the Romans:

> For I am sure that neither death, nor life, nor angels, nor principalities, nor things present, nor things to come, nor powers, nor height, nor depth, nor anything else in all creation, will be able to separate us from the love of God in Christ Jesus our Lord. (Rom 8:38–39)

God gives special strength to Christians who shed their blood in bearing witness to their faith. The world has always been awed by the fortitude of martyrs who withstood trials for the love of God. St. Cyprian described one such scene: "The crowd of onlookers wondered to see an unearthly battle, and Christ's servants fighting erect, undaunted in speech, with souls unmoved, and strength divine." They were valiant in the ultimate battle.[85]

Not every Christian is called to martyrdom. But everyone baptized has the duty to bear witness to his or her faith in words and deeds. Faith is not to be kept hidden, but is meant to be shared with others. By definition a Christian is a missionary, called to be another Christ wherever life finds him or her. In a world characterized by a "cancel culture" and the "tyranny of relativism," to borrow the expression of Pope Emeritus Benedict XVI, proclaiming our faith can be unpopular. More and more people are allergic to the moral truth, and yet we have to speak the truth even if it is difficult to do so. Hence, living our faith requires fortitude. "Be sober, be watchful. Your adversary the devil prowls around like a roaring lion, seeking some one to devour. Resist him, firm in your faith [*fortes in fide*]" (1 Pt 5:8–9).

Recall the old rite of the sacrament of confirmation. The candidate was struck lightly with a slap on the cheek by the bishop as a symbol of fortitude, reminding the new "soldier of Christ" to be brave in spreading and defending the Faith. Liturgical reforms may have removed or toned down this knightly gesture, but the call to courage remains.

Without reference to eternal life, fortitude risks falling into nihilism, where the *effort* rather than the *end* is taken as the ultimate good. At the end of the day what counts is not whether the struggle is easy or hard, but the real good or the truth for which we toil. The rectitude of hope lies in the fact that it corresponds to this reality. Hope for eternal life is a gift and it is intrinsic to Christian fortitude.[86]

Supernatural fortitude has an uncanny ability to bear contradictions that, for natural motives, a person might try to avoid. Christian sacrifice operates on a higher plane than human struggle. A person who strives to become a saint sees the difficulties as opportunities to expiate his or her sins, to make amends, to atone for the offenses of others, and to co-redeem with Christ. Christian mortification is senseless in a secular world but an instrument to grow in holiness for pious souls. If hardships are conquered by the natural person in order to attain human plenitude, the same are overcome by the child of God to achieve Christian perfection.

Reflecting on the supernatural gift of fortitude, Pope Francis said that the virtue helps us to remain faithful not only in big things but also in our habitual occupations. It gives us the strength to do God's will in spite of our own natural weakness and shortcomings. It sustains us through the fatigues and trials of life so that we do not get discouraged and fall into despair. When we feel tired or burdened in our journey, fortitude refreshes us and guides our steps with renewed enthusiasm.[87]

St. Paul extols the virtues of a good soldier as a model of Christian conduct (see 2 Tm 2:3–4). We may not have to literally take up arms, but the Sacred Scriptures mince no words to tell us that life on earth is a spiritual battle in which we need to wrestle, stand firm, resist evil, and put on the armor of God (see Eph 6:13). Final perseverance is the most important gift for which we need to ask the Lord, so that at the sunset of life we may be able to say with the Apostle of the Gentiles, "I have fought the good fight, I have finished the race, I have kept the faith" (2 Tm 4:7).

CHAPTER 4

The Virtue of Temperance

The front cover of this book shows a masterpiece by the Italian Renaissance painter Piero del Pollaiolo (Florence, 1443–1496) depicting a woman pouring a small amount of water into a basin filled with wine. Her act of diluting the alcohol symbolizes restraint. The white and blue colors of the water stand for purity. She's wearing green to signify control of human excesses. Her long brown sleeves and the cloth draped over her lap indicate earth. The message is clear: the woman is in the world tainted by sin and corruption, but she does an act of purification. We have a fallen nature given to self-indulgence, but we can and must practice moderation. The lady of course is an allegory of the cardinal virtue of temperance.

Temperance is basically about moderation. It is a general virtue, since reason governs all pleasurable experiences of man. But considered in a more restricted sense, temperance is a special virtue to the extent that reason curbs sensual pleasures, especially the senses of taste and touch. Bodily contact tends to arouse pleasure or cause pain more intensely than any other human activity. Temperance regulates the passions that draw us toward sensibly pleasurable goods, as well as feelings of sadness due to the privation of such pleasures.[1]

The notion of temperance is semantically related to the "golden mean," a moral principle propounded by ancient Greek thinkers. One of the Delphic maxims carved on the Temple of Apollo at Delphi in Greece says, "Nothing in excess." The same idea is expressed by the English proverb, "Too much of anything is good for nothing."

Innate Tendency

We are all born with basic tendencies, which are not specific hobbies like rock climbing, pastry cooking, poetry writing, or anything that certain people may rave about but others find unappealing. Basic desires are deep inclinations embedded in our human nature, and there is no need to prove their existence.[2] God created us, chiefly, with two innate desires: the urge to eat and drink, and sexual attraction. As creatures, our most natural operations involve self-preservation (we eat to satisfy our hunger and drink to quench our thirst) and the preservation of the human species (we tend to sexual union to beget children).[3]

Our desire to stay alive and transmit life are instinctive; these proclivities operate on the unconscious level. To preserve its existence is the first good of every creature. Our foremost desire is the desire to live. We are hardly aware of it when this tendency to permanence is satisfied. It is something given and constant, like the beating of our heart.

Yet these same survival instincts manifest in the form of appetites that operate on the conscious level in three areas: concupiscible, irascible, and spiritual (will). Pain, for example, is nature's signal on the conscious level that we are unwell and that something has to be done about it. Likewise, thirst and hunger are natural but conscious tendencies. We know when we need to eat and drink, and when we are satisfied there is a reward: pleasure.[4]

One of the greatest ironies in human life is the fact that our powers of self-preservation—eating for personal nourishment and sex to propagate the human species—can also be the roots of self-destruction. Because these forces are closely allied to the deepest human urge toward being, they are unsurpassed in destructive potential when they go berserk.[5] Desires for higher goods like truth and beauty are certainly more noble, but they are less intense than bodily appetites because the sensible goods, especially food, drink, and sex, are so fundamental and necessary to human existence.[6] If we can control our strongest desires, it should be easier to manage the less powerful ones.

Even reading a book, listening to music, or praying can bring pleasure and comfort. People enjoy acquiring new knowledge and having intellectual insights such that a person can go overboard in satisfying his or her mental appetites. It is one thing to read books; vain curiosity is quite another. Heartfelt consolations help us pray, but to seek feelings excessively is to risk reducing prayer to a mere sentimental experience. Hence, the virtue of temperance must also moderate the spiritual pleasures and mental appetites.

Yet bodily pleasures tend to be more vehement than spiritual enjoyments for three reasons: we easily know them, they trigger bodily reactions, and they alleviate physical troubles.[7] Therefore, the primary object of temperance is carnal pleasures (sensible and material). The palate and libido are a person's most primeval impulses, his or her most powerful urges, so it is harder to keep them in check[8] than other innate tendencies we have. No human drives are as potent as eating, drinking, and the sexual act; no other experience is more riveting than what corresponds to these organic functions.

However, if we reduce our life to carnal pleasures, we begin to act like beasts. Precisely, we share with nonrational animals the appetites and pleasures derived from food, drink, and sex.[9] Dogs and cats mate instinctively (without love and courtship) and eat when fed (more or less), following a stimulus-response pattern. But men and women are not supposed to behave like the canine and feline. We humans should not act by sheer instinct but must regulate our passions. One is brute and savage who pampers his or her cravings for food and sex in a way that is crude, wanton, and unrestrained.

Rational Being

We must rise above sheer animal life, for we are rational beings who unite in our own nature both the spiritual and material worlds. Created in the "image and likeness of God" (Gn 1:27), the human person occupies a unique place in the order of creation. We are the only visible beings on earth created for our own sake,[10] the only ones called to share in the intimacy of divine life by knowing and loving our Creator. Endowed with reason and free will, we possess human dignity and personal honor. No other living thing in this world has a sense of morality, respect, shame, decorum, etiquette, propriety, and sensibility.

The proximate subject of the virtue of temperance understood in its strict sense is the concupiscible appetite, which is subject to a person's reason and will. If we have an irascible appetite that triggers passions like hope, despair, fear, daring, or anger, depending on whether an arduous good is attained or not, threatened, or secured, so also we have a concupiscible appetite that produces passions like love, hatred, desire, aversion, joy, or sadness, depending on whether or not we get to enjoy a pleasurable good.[11]

We can appreciate better the virtue of temperance against the backdrop of human indiscipline. Moral disorders often stem from a lack of self-control: lust, gluttony, outburst, drunkenness, carousal, and the like. But also others: immodesty, curiosity, impatience, boastfulness, or extravagance. All these acts or vices imply overindulgence that needs moderation. Temperance functions like a levee or dike built along the sea of passions or river of desires, to channel its flow and prevent it from overflowing. Similarly, intemperance is akin to dike breaches that can lead to catastrophic flooding of appetites, which submerge us in a debris of licentiousness and sensuality.

If temperance bridles our tendency to excesses, what constitutes an excess? How much is too much? Generally, when a person keeps on eating despite being full, needs to take a breather before the next bite, or feels heavy once the meal is over, he is probably overstuffed. Determining how much to eat, though, is a little tricky. What is enough for a little girl is meager for a construction worker. Several factors like body mass, age, gender, nutrition, or metabolism mean that temperance does not give a one-size-fits-all measure of food intake. The same can be said of drink and, in some ways, the sexual faculty.

From the moral point of view, the proper end of something is the rule and measure of whatever is directed to that end. The sexual faculty is naturally ordained to the conjugal union of a man and a woman in a covenant of love, as well as the procreation of children. Hence, chastity is based on the nature and ends of marriage. From here it is easy to glean why adultery ("my spouse is not enough") and contraception ("sex is good, but no child") are immoral. They are forms of sexual intemperance.

Health and bodily nourishment are the proper ends of eating and drinking. So consuming beyond what is needed for good health is gluttony and insobriety. One more bite of chocolate or an extra glass of wine is fine once in a while; temperance is not about starving oneself or quantified abstinence. But we know when it is time to put the fork down. The Stoic philosopher Seneca (c. 4 BC–AD 65) denounced the custom of those who "vomit that they may eat, and they eat that they may fetch it up again,"[12] alluding to the corrupt Roman custom of grand banquets characterized by lavish, exotic meals and a drinking binge in a large dining hall or sprawling garden, "graced" by dancers, acrobats, musicians, jugglers, and masseuses.

Balance and Equilibrium

The definition of temperance as restraint of appetites is only partially true and runs the risk of reducing the virtue to something negative, a form of repression. In reality, temperance has a positive meaning that implies a habitual disposition to order our desires. The temperate person does not only dominate his or her passions, but orients them in such a way that all his or her instincts and impulses are at the service of the whole person. St. Paul expresses this idea when he says that God put harmony among the different members of the human body (see 1 Cor 12:24).[13]

Temperance must at times favor—not curb—a person's instinctive tendencies, as when the disequilibrium stems not from its force and frenzy but from coldness, frigidity, or indifference.[14] Someone who gorges on food is intemperate by excess, while vanity can lead another to eat too little and therefore be intemperate by defect. If a man treats his wife as a mere object of pleasure, he is intemperate by excess. But similarly, a person who refuses the marital act when it is reasonable is intemperate, but by defect, for sex is part of the deal: it is a marital obligation.

Derived from Latin *temperare* (to mingle in due proportions, to qualify),

> *Temperance* is the moral virtue that moderates the attraction of pleasures and provides balance in the use of created goods. It ensures the will's mastery over instincts and keeps desires within the limits of what is honorable. The temperate person directs the sensitive appetites toward what is good and maintains a healthy discretion.[15]

He or she eats enough, drinks enough, sleeps enough, rests enough, reads enough, and enjoys anything good in just the right amount.[16] Balance. Equilibrium. Order. That's the key, neither lavish nor inadequate.

Temperance invites us to look deep into our inner self and set things right. We turn toward ourselves in a way that either preserves us (selfless) or ruins us (selfish).[17] It is a lifelong task to align our passions with right reason, putting them back on track each time they deviate due to our inherent weakness and wounded nature. This is the most profound meaning of the Latin word *temperantia* and its closest Greek equivalent, *sophrosyne*, which means "directing reason." The virtue integrates the different parts of the whole person, body and soul, and reins in the tendency of the lower appetites to go wild. Inner harmony is achieved, allowing the person to mature. We may feel the pinch caused by self-denial, especially if it means giving up something we like. But it is worth the sacrifice. We grow as a person only if we strive to be the master of our passions, not the servant.

Pleasure and Human Good

Our innate tendencies point to deep human needs, and so they refer to something radically good for us. We take it for granted that we like to eat well and stay in tip-top shape, to be in relationships and marry, to study and be learned, to pray and attend church services, to work and earn money, to own property and secure our future, to have friends and socialize, to rest and enjoy hobbies, and so forth. From the theological point of view, these basic desires—shorn of selfish motives—are a sign of the person's participation in the creative work of God through an inner impulse inscribed in the nature of each individual.[18] Even the pleasure that accompanies eating, drinking, and the sexual act are God-given. They are good per se, for nothing evil comes out of the hands of God. Aristotle and Aquinas both affirm that virtue consists not only in doing the right thing for the right reason, but also with the right emotions and passions. You certainly do well if you enjoy a hearty Mediterranean dish. It is perfectly alright to savor your favorite meal: you are being temperate. If a married person is passionate about performing the marital act with whom he or she truly loves, that is expected. He or she is being temperate. Temperance is not meant to eliminate passions and emotions but to order them according to reason.[19] Pleasure in general is the repose of the appetite in the good, and it perfects the operations to that end. Simply stated, we enjoy doing certain good acts, and the pleasure we experience motivates us to perform better. We tend to have a better grasp of what we read if we like the topic or the author. We usually eat well if the platter served is our favorite. These are appropriate pleasures, they do not hinder reason, they are not bad. But bodily pleasures can go beyond what is reasonable, especially if they are unrestrained or sought for their own sake.[20]

Morality is based not only on a person's action and intention, but also his or her emotions and passions. Virtue concerns not just our acts and desires but also our feelings. Sound strange? Can we be held accountable for how we feel about things? If I'm upset and angry at my brother for not paying what he owes me on time, am I doing wrong? If you crave raspberry velvet cake as you drive near your favorite pastry shop, does that sentiment morally matter? In other words, can we be praised or blamed for our emotional responses to events and situations? You might be surprised that the answer is "yes."

Emotions are not deliberate decisions, but they are often the roots of our actions. Our feelings are reflexive (that is, unthinking) but not totally passive or neutral. They can and should be influenced by our reason and will. If a person is sexually aroused in an inappropriate way, he or she does not commit evil if the passion is not self-provoked. But if he or she dwells on that disordered passion and wallows in that feeling, then this person is at fault. We have a situation equivalent to the sin against the ninth commandment, confirmed by Jesus when he says, "Every one who looks at a woman lustfully has already committed adultery with her in his heart" (Mt 5:28). We are also culpable if we place ourselves in compromising situations. It is not advisable to hang out with heavy drinkers if you do not want to relapse into alcoholism. Nor is it a good idea to recall or talk about events that reopen old wounds and fan deep-seated anger. Remember the admonition of Jesus, "Every one who is angry with his brother shall be liable to judgment" (Mt 5:22). Here the Lord rebuked not so much an unjust angry act but an unjust angry feeling and desire.

Indeed, it is proper to speak of virtuous desires and upright emotions. Our feelings, too, need to be moderated and tempered.[21] If the brave person is someone who has fears but manages to regulate them, the temperate person is he or she who has disordered tendencies but takes charge of them. Of course, external acts carry more weight than mere desires and passions. Moral theology teaches us that the morality of a human act depends mainly on the moral object and intentions of the agent. Yet emotions do have moral significance, either for good or evil. They fall within the purview of the cardinal virtue of temperance.

Contrary Vices[22]

1. Insensibility[23]

Two vices are opposed to the virtue of temperance: *insensibility* and *intemperance*. Pleasures are part of our life. As we said earlier, the satisfaction that goes with eating, drinking, and sex is inscribed in our nature. These things are God-given and so they are essentially good, something meant to facilitate essential human activities.

Imagine if the simple act of eating were unpleasant instead of delectable: many people would soon become emaciated. They would have to be coaxed to eat. So too, the sexual act comes with pleasure that serves as a stimulus for men and women to willingly become parents and form a family. Otherwise, if the use of the sexual faculty were arduous rather than enjoyable, society would have to come up with all sorts of incentives just so couples would pair, beget children, and populate the earth. God knew better.

Insensibility is the error of disregarding what is necessary for our well-being. Anyone who rejects pleasure to the extent of omitting one's fundamental duties as regards life, health, family, fidelity, and the like falls into sin. To act against the natural order is morally wrong. We ought to appreciate and put to good use what God gave us. Despising pleasure is tantamount to disdaining something authentically human. Pleasure goes with appetite, which is embedded in our physical, emotional, psychological, spiritual, and emotional constitution.

In the history of Christianity, heresies were spread by the Manichaeists (third century AD) and the Catharists (twelfth–fourteenth century AD), who believed in the dualist principle of good (the spiritual world) and evil (the world of matter). The human body is a source of depravity, they said, and is everything associated with it, including sex, marriage, procreation, and maternity. This is a rigorist and spurious teaching.

The truth is that we are not pure spirits like the angels, nor pure matter, a mere aggregate of organs, muscles, and nerves, but a composite of body and soul, corporal and spiritual. Our body partakes of the dignity of the whole person, especially of the spiritual dimension. Thus, it is important to reaffirm the radical goodness of the human body, along with its pleasures and sensibilities. Besides, the human body has been redeemed by Christ, who "became flesh and dwelt among us" (Jn 1:14). In his Letter to the Corinthians, St. Paul gave them an important reminder and urged them to stay pure: "Do you not know that your body is the temple of the Holy Spirit? . . . So glorify God in your body" (1 Cor 6:19–20).

2. Intemperance[24]

If *insensibility* is numbness to pleasures, *intemperance* is over-indulgence in them. Two extremes, like the far west and the far east. Intemperance is unbridled concupiscence. Aquinas compared it to a small child who likes base things, grows headstrong, and needs to be disciplined. Just as the child requires guidance from his tutor, so appetite must be regulated by reason.

We know how spoiled brats are. Pampered by their parents, they exhibit behavioral problems. They cannot be told "no" or "wait." The kids may have lots of toys, but they are never satisfied. They do not fix their bed or brush their teeth. You have to bribe them just to do a little thing. "Thank you" is not in their vocabulary, for spoiled children are self-centered. Then there is whining, crying, pounding, breath-holding, and so forth. Intemperance is personified by the little rascals who lack self-discipline.

But a small child that is well behaved is admirable. There is something angelic in an innocent, fair, and dutiful little girl or boy. He or she does his or her homework, takes care of younger siblings, knows what is right and wrong, tells the truth, is polite and well mannered, is friendly with other kids, and speaks politely to adults. A fine, well-bred child embodies, so to speak, the virtue of temperance.

When we try to satisfy our natural desires like hunger or thirst fair and square, we enjoy with moderation. But when we give free rein to our whims and caprice, we go overboard and violate the dictates of reason. The vice of intemperance is most disgraceful on two counts. First, it is most repugnant to human excellence, since we wallow in pleasures common to men and beasts. Second, it contradicts most the beauty and splendor of human beings, darkening the light of reason. Sensuality has a blinding effect; intemperance is slavish.

Integral Parts

The cardinal virtue of temperance has two integral parts or elements necessary for the virtue to be present, namely, the *sense of shame*, whereby a person shuns anything base or disgraceful due to lack of self-control, and the *sense of honor*, whereby a person loves the beauty of moderation. Of all the human virtues, temperance sets the highest horizontal bar of decorum and propriety, just as intemperance points to what is most shameful, mean, ignoble, and reprobate.[25]

1. Sense of Shame[26]

Shame (Latin *verecundia*) is the fear of disgrace from reproach due to our wrongdoing. Just as the good things we do deserve honor, the wicked deeds we commit bring disgrace. We shrink back, as it were, from doing anything that no sensible person can take pride in. Thus, a decent person who, in an unguarded moment, loses self-control by yelling or cursing in public would feel regret and humiliation once he or she regains composure. People who talk nonsense, do stupid things, or confess secrets when they are drunk feel embarrassed and ashamed when they sober up and recover. An employee who is caught watching YouTube videos during office hours will likely look awkward and abashed. Whoever is guilty of a foul act will recoil out of disgrace, says Aquinas.

Other animals do not have a sense of shame; they are what they are, ruled by instinct. Not so in the case of humans, since we are rational beings. As we have said, when we let our lower appetites get the better of us, we begin to behave like animals. Therefore, *shamefacedness* fosters balance, moderation, and integrity. The fear of being regarded as shameless, mean, base, low-down, and vicious leads us to behave well and to give a good example to others; or to apologize if the shameful act has already been committed. There is no use crying over spilled milk, but a person can straighten things up and do damage control. Temperance rests on self-respect and personal pride. Shamefacedness is a healthy sense of one's true worth as a dignified individual and the desire to preserve that image of a well-ordered life.[27]

Strictly speaking, what causes ignominy and scandal are vicious deeds, not bad desires. The very idea of being embarrassed holds us back from acting immoderately. But a person can be devious and still avoid public ridicule by simply hiding his or her actions. Aquinas notes besides that we tend to feel more shame in the presence of people who know us well than in the company of strangers. We let pass and easily forget the stupidities or *faux pas* we commit in the city squares where pedestrians and tourists hardly notice us. But we are more affected if our blunders happen right before our close family and friends. We fluster, wish to hide, or even "die of shame."

How about the word *shameless*? Well, it refers to those unfortunate folks who are so immersed in vice, so used to moral corruption that they have lost the sense of shame. They may even boast of having shortchanged a client in a business deal, flirted with a married person, or cheated on a professional board exam. Shamelessness is a form of moral numbness born of a deformed conscience and deeply entrenched vices.

Taken in a strict sense, shamefacedness is not a virtue. Fearing ill-repute falls short of the perfection of virtue. We do not really become good if all we do is avoid giving a bad example or the wrong impression. A virtuous life consists in doing positive acts of service, kindness, loyalty, diligence, chastity, and so forth. Besides, feeling ashamed is not a conscious choice but a spontaneous feeling. But taken in a broad sense, shamefacedness may be regarded as a virtue; it is a laudable passion for it does foster honesty and breed good behaviors. A healthy sense of guilt certainly helps us to watch our steps, so to speak, and to be mindful of others.

2. Sense of Honor[28]

Together with the *sense of shame*, the *sense of honor* or *honesty* constitutes an integral part of the cardinal virtue of temperance. *Honesty* here does not mean truth-telling, but rather beauty of the soul. The English word that best expresses this notion is *decency* or *decorum*. What is honest or decorous has excellence of character; it abhors anything that's unbecoming of the dignity of the human person.

When people say, "She is a very beautiful woman" or, "He is such a good-looking guy," they generally refer to ordered physical traits: symmetrical face, nice hair, smooth skin, lustrous eyes, broad shoulders, slender waist, and so on. Aquinas writes of proportioned limbs and ruddy radiance.[29] Similarly, inner beauty implies order. We appreciate the beauty of a well-ordered character, a life of moral integrity. An honest person is temperate, moderates his or her passions, and has a well-balanced personality.

Our sense of honor goes beyond the realm of self. How we practice self-control impacts the people around us. Temperance means giving personal witness to what is authentically human and rejecting subhuman behavior. When we moderate our desires and act with a sense of honor, our external affairs and social dealings reflect that interior harmony.[30] Thus, the sense of honor is the same as spiritual beauty.[31]

Subjective Parts and Contrary Vices

The subjective parts of the virtue of temperance are aspects or species of the virtue and are distinguished according to the objects that they govern. In a way, different forms of temperance can be identified, depending on whether it regulates the pleasures of nourishment (eating and drinking) or procreation (sex).

1. Abstinence[32]

Abstinence is the ability to control excessive and unhealthy eating. But just because a person cuts down on calories does not mean he or she is doing something praiseworthy. The act or virtue of abstinence implies regulation by reason, meaning that we should eat the right food, in the right amount, and at the proper time. In other words, abstinence is basically prudent eating, including the joy of having a good meal.[33]

One of the subjective parts of temperance, abstinence is a special virtue that is important for a simple reason: eating food is a natural good that is pleasurable, so much so that people tend to overindulge in savory cuisines. Hence, the effort to rein in one's food cravings, the act of abstaining from food, especially meat, helps us tame our sensuality. Why meat? Because we are an omnivorous animal. We love to eat beef, pork, lamb, turkey, or chicken. Cutting down or giving up the object of craving can help promote spiritual well-being.

Strictly, abstinence is eating with due regard for the people who live with us (being a good example to others), for our own selves (to respect, not shame ourselves), and for our own health needs (to know our capacity and limits). If these parameters are clear, it matters little what we eat and how much we eat, says St. Augustine. The measure of self-restraint is not fixed but depends on a person's circumstances. The mean of the virtue of abstinence is not based on quantity but on what is reasonable.[34]

One concrete act of abstinence is fasting, a virtue with a threefold purpose: to bridle the lusts of the flesh, to foster spiritual contemplation, and to atone for our sins. In a sense, everyone is bound by natural law to observe fasting: it is a dictate of reason. But it is also a precept in the Catholic Church, with specific norms regarding the time and manner of this ascetical practice.[35] The 1983 Code of Canon Law (canons 1249–1253) binds all Catholics from age eighteen to fifty-nine to the law of fasting and abstinence (unless they are exempt for valid reasons) on Ash Wednesday and Good Friday. Abstinence from meat is to be observed by all the faithful (age fourteen years or older) on all Fridays of the year, except when a Friday is a liturgical solemnity. Substitute acts of piety are allowed.

Fasting and abstinence are the primary forms of asceticism, and they are linked to the notion of *hilaritas mentis* (cheerfulness of the heart). Offhand, this idea sounds strange. Privation often leads to suffering and sadness, not comfort and joy. But it is the Lord Jesus who admonished us, saying, "[W]hen you fast, do not look dismal, like the hypocrites," who appear unkempt to show that they are making sacrifices (Mt 6:16). Fasting is meritorious only if it is a sincere practice, not motivated by the desire to be praised by others.

Gluttony[36]

Gluttony is the vice opposed to the virtue of abstinence. It is the inordinate desire and craving for food. Food is not bad, but its abuse is. The Gospel states that "not what goes into the mouth defiles a man" (Mt 15:11). If you see a chubby fellow at a deli café eating a large stack of pancakes, served with bacon, egg muffins, maple syrup, a sausage combo, banana slices, and hazelnuts, you might think, "Here is a gorger and hefty eater with zero self-control." Be careful, do not judge!

The evil of gluttony lies in an excessive desire for pleasure in eating, not in the quantity we eat. This is a little tricky, for how we act, in a sense, betrays our motives. But Aquinas notes that a person may eat, for example, due to a mistaken idea of nutritional needs. He or she is not a glutton for this reason, but only when the person "knowingly" overeats for the experience of pleasure.

The human appetite is twofold. On the one hand, we have a *natural appetite* (vegetal) that includes hunger and thirst. This tendency is not ruled by reason, and so there is no right and wrong here. We have little control over the timing of when to feel starved or dehydrated. On the other hand, we have a *sensitive appetite* where gluttony is possible through concupiscence. Pope Gregory the Great (sixth century AD) listed gluttony as one of the seven deadly sins, and he defined it succinctly as the vice that involves eating too soon, too delicately, too costly, too greedily, and too much.[37]

In effect, the glutton eats the choicest foodstuffs, seeks dishes overzealously, or eats more than he or she should.[38] This person also tends to eat hastily as if in a rush, devours every morsel on the plate, and eats voraciously, ignoring table manners. Snacking at odd hours, fussing about the sumptuous six-course meal at the bar-lounge of a celebrity chef: the list continues on and on. But the common thread of all these acts is the concupiscence of sensory pleasures (*delictationes*) associated with food and drink.[39]

Overeating may be seen by contemporary society as a bad health choice associated with obesity and health risks. Instead of blaming food advertisements and gourmet ads, practice self-mastery! As a moral issue, gluttony is a capital sin, for it gives rise to other disorders. Aquinas lists the daughters of gluttony: dullness of mind (deadened wit and understanding), unseemly and excessive joy (frivolity, indecency), loquaciousness (unbridled speech), scurrility (vulgarity, coarse language, foul mouth) and uncleanness (vomiting, lust, seminal emission). "When the belly is full to bursting with food and drink, debauchery knocks at the door," wrote Thomas à Kempis, a fourteenth-century German-Dutch monk and author of the Christian classic *The Imitation of Christ*.[40]

2. Sobriety[41]

The word *sobriety* comes from the Latin *bria* (feminine noun, *bria, briae*), meaning wine vessel. Hence, *bria* is a liquid measure, and from there is derived the English term *sobriety*. A sober person is one who observes the proper measure of drink. The *virtue of sobriety* is aimed at moderating our alcohol intake, because intoxicants can be beneficial when taken moderately, yet harmful when taken in excess. Getting inebriated hinders the use of reason in a way that is even worse than gluttony.

We appreciate better the virtue of sobriety if we remember that its opposite vice, drunkenness, is the cause of so much disorder, violence, and strife. In contrast, the experience of alcoholics who overcome their addiction shows the benefits of being sober. There is a sense of freedom, improved mental focus, healthier relationships, quality sleep and rest, decreased health risks, greater emotional stability, increased self-confidence, and deeper spirituality.

The issue with alcoholic drink is not its use but its abuse. First Timothy 5:23 even recommends wine, but with moderation: "No longer drink any water, but use a little wine for the sake of your stomach and your frequent ailments." At the wedding at Cana Jesus converted water into wine (Jn 2:1–11), and wine is used in the sacrament of the Eucharist. On a practical level, alcoholic beverages, taken in the proper amount, can help people relax and can cheer up social gatherings. The world of wine and spirits is an essential part of human culture.

But taking liquor is not a good idea for someone prone to binge drinking, or who has taken a vow not to drink, or who causes scandal to others. In other words, while it is not wrong to drink, the circumstances matter. It can be vicious accidentally, says Aquinas. The key is prudence. You know yourself, you know your limits, and you know what is proper. An extra glass of wine may be OK once in a while, but not always. If you have been through a recovery and detoxication program, even just a sip of whiskey or vodka is off limits. If your kids are around at a cocktail party, be mindful of setting a good example. And be sure you are alcohol-free when you drive. In sum, pay heed to the label on beers and spirits: drink responsibly!

Drunkenness[42]

Opposed to sobriety is *drunkenness*, which eclipses the intellect that, together with the will, forms the basis human dignity. Stories abound of what people do when inebriated: they get emotional, feel strong attraction, spill out secrets, cavort with strangers, dance shamelessly, lose their belongings, and leave lousy social media posts. Getting intoxicated is like renouncing self-control and unleashing the beast within us. Drunkenness preys upon the nerves and the brain; and given the psychosomatic nature of man, it leads to an impotence of the will, weakening our ability to ward off temptations.[43]

But there is more. The evil of drunkenness goes beyond impairment of the mind. For instance, we can lose the use of our faculties due to anesthetics as part of a medical procedure, yet this is obviously not sinful. Ultimately, the immorality of drunkenness rests on the pursuit of an inferior pleasure. The person is more culpable the more willful is his or her getting drunk, the more systematic is the vice, and the longer is the state of intoxication.[44]

Alcoholism is not just a moral but also a pathological problem that gets worse over time and can damage the liver, brain, and heart. The social impact of alcoholism is incalculable: more road accidents, higher health care costs, greater productivity losses, increased theft and violence, and higher incidence of divorce and other social disturbances. To the extent possible, anyone who suffers alcoholism should seek professional help for proper diagnosis, treatment, and rehabilitation.

3. Chastity and Purity[45]

Chastity is the virtue that moderates sexual pleasures. The Latin adjective *castus* (cut off, separated) is linked to the verb *castigo* (chastise, reprimand, correct) and is used by Aristotle in *Nicomachean Ethics*[46] to say that reason chastises concupiscence in the same way that a child needs to be disciplined.

A subjective part of temperance, chastity is rooted in human dignity. A person's sexual drive is stronger than his nutritional appetite, so it needs greater restraint. The more a person falls into lust, the more overpowering the concupiscence, the darker the mind, the weaker the will, the more blunt the conscience. Unless chastity intervenes, the person tends to lower him- or herself to the level of brutish instincts.

There is something divine in the human seed.[47] Sex is God's great gift to humanity: it is not a "necessary evil," but radically good. Hence, chastity is not meant to weaken the power of the sexual faculty but harness it for a good end. This virtue has nothing to do with a dull personality and boring life. Chastity receives bad publicity, for it is often seen as a repression of a deep human need. On the contrary, it is about liberation from bondage, not repression of desires. "Chastity means the successful integration of sexuality within the person and thus the inner unity of man in his bodily and spiritual being."[48] It requires self-discipline and training in human freedom.

Sex is a sign and expression of our capacity to love and vocation to love. In his catecheses called *Man and Woman He Created Them: A Theology of the Body*, St. John Paul II leads us to a deep understanding of human sexuality as a sign of fecundity, procreation, and the *nuptial meaning of the body*, that is, self-donation as the intrinsic purpose of sexuality.[49] The person becomes a gift in that relationship of conjugal love. In the couple's mutual self-giving, sexuality acquires a truly human quality[50] and becomes a tool to build a civilization of love.

Every person ought to live chastity according to his or her state in life: man or woman, single or married, young or old, lay or clergy, rich or poor, healthy or sick. Who says that this virtue is only for the young and unmarried? A wedding, for example, is not a license for couples to watch lewd shows. Anything that can tarnish a little child can stain an adult just as much. For the unmarried, chastity means total abstinence from sex. For husband and wife, it means that all sexual acts must reflect their marital love that is total, exclusive, indissoluble, and open to life.

Part of chastity is the virtue of *purity* (*pudicia*), which takes its name from *pudor* (shame). Purity concerns the most shameful things, that is, venereal pleasures. So much so that even the conjugal act, which is good in itself, is not bereft of shame, affirms St. Augustine.[51] Temperance regulates not only the sexual act per se (lovemaking), but also its outward signs like touches, kisses, and looks. Purity moderates what society calls making out, petting, necking, caressing, and other acts that are short of vaginal intercourse but arouse passion, "turning on" a person sexually. Purity is part of chastity, but the two words are often used interchangeably, both referring to sexual temperance.

a. Bogus Anthropology

To a large extent, contemporary society has fallen prey to Freudian psychology. Human behavior, we are made to believe, is the product of the unconscious. All psychic activities tend to seek pleasure and avoid pain. The principle of pleasure is the driving force of our *libido*, the sexual instinct or *eros*. There is a tinge of determinism in Freud's pseudo-philosophy, for it traces the human act to the instinctive in the person, leaving us bereft of freedom. Eroticism would then be the most "natural" thing for everyone.

Freudian logic is built on a bogus anthropology that animalizes the human person.[52] Peter Kreeft, philosophy professor at Boston College, has exposed the gross sexual reductionism of Sigmund Freud. As an atheist, Freud reduces God to a human dream. As a materialist, he reduces the person to his or her body, the body to animal instinct, instinct to sexual desire, and desire to genital sex. All these are oversimplifications.[53]

We are rational creatures endowed with the capacity to know and to choose. Embedded in our minds and hearts is the desire for what is true, good, and beautiful—ultimately it is the yearning for the absolute good, God himself. St. Paul VI reminds us that

> [m]an, created to God's image and likeness, is not just flesh and blood; the sexual instinct is not all that he has; man has also, and preeminently, understanding, choice, freedom, and thanks to these powers he is, and must remain, the chief work of creation; they give him mastery over his physical, mental and emotional appetites.[54]

In a hedonistic world, the person loses self-worth and is treated as an object of sensual pleasure. Sex is sought as a pastime, devoid of stable commitments. No marriage. No babies. No promises. Men and women hook up quite casually and just as casually break up to change partners, making a plaything out of sex. They use rather than love each other, in utter disregard of human dignity and the sanctity of love and life. When satisfaction fades away, the person is set aside, the way obsolete gadgets and appliances are scrapped.

In his book *The Closing of the American Mind*, Allan Bloom, professor of social thought at the University of Chicago, exposed the deep cultural crisis in American society. One chapter zeroes in on promiscuity among young people:

> "Sexual liberation presented itself as a bold affirmation of the senses and of . . . natural impulse against our puritanical heritage. . . . From the early sixties on there was a gradual testing of the limits on sexual expression, and they melted away . . . without anybody" noticing it. The disapproval of parents and teachers of youngsters' sleeping together was easily overcome. The moral inhibitions, the fear of disease, the risk of pregnancy, the consequences of premarital intercourse . . . everything that stood in its way suddenly was no longer there." Female modesty was gradually phased out and lovemaking became a "primary activity."[55]

America is not the entire world, but much of what Allan Bloom described has happened in most liberal Western societies.

b. Lust[56]

Lust is sexual debauchery. Though in a broad sense lust is any kind of excess (see Gal 5:19). it chiefly applies to venereal pleasures. Not all sexual enjoyment is evil, for as we have said earlier, there is a licit use of sex and its pleasures. But the disordered use of the sexual faculty is immoral.

Since the object of lust—sexual pleasures—is connatural to man and is very intense, it gives rise to a chain of evils. Therefore, lust is a capital sin. Aquinas points out that the higher faculties (the reason and the will) are grievously hindered in their acts by the lower appetite (concupiscible) due to the *vice of lust*. As a result, the person falls into what he calls the daughters of lust: blindness of mind, thoughtlessness, inconstancy, rashness, self-love, hatred of God, love of this world, and abhorrence or despair of a future world.[57]

People given to the pleasures of the flesh can hardly make sound judgments and good moral choices. They are at the mercy of temptations because they have little strength to resist them. Their unchaste life is shown in their sloth, passivity, anger, gluttony, arrogance, materialism, and irreverence.

Theologians identify various forms of lust when it is a consummated external act: fornication, adultery, incest, rape, and sodomy, each of which has its own specific malice. Really anything lascivious is lustful: self-abuse, pornography, voyeurism, prostitution, lewd shows, seduction, immodesty, and the like. Not all unchastity, though, is visible. A person can commit lust even just internally, through impure desire, imagination, or memory. The ninth commandment of the Decalogue bares the depravity of impure thoughts and desires, even if the equivalent external sins are usually more grievous.

St. Paul tells us why sins against chastity are particularly grave:

> Every other sin which a man commits is outside the body; but the immoral man sins against his own body. Do you not know that your body is a temple of the Holy Spirit within you, which you have from God? You are not your own; you

were bought with a price. So glorify God in your body. (1 Cor 6:18–20)

Potential Parts and Contrary Vices

Temperance has a series of secondary virtues which resemble but are not exactly identical to it as the principal virtue. As we shall see, temperance is not just moderation of pleasures in food, drink, and sex. It has related or annexed virtues that regulate other human desires and external conduct.

1. Continence[58]

Continence is abstention from all venereal pleasures. Whoever avoids all sexual pleasures is a *virgin*, a state that one may choose in order to have total devotion and undivided attention to God, and which implies integrity of the flesh, free from all sexual experience. This is called *perfect continence*.[59]

Taken in a strict sense, continence is a potential part of temperance that denotes resistance to all evil desires experienced as a vehement passion. St. Paul listed it as one of the fruits of the Holy Spirit (see Gal 5:23). Reason stands firm so that a person does not succumb to temptations. As its very name suggests, continence involves an act of curbing ("containing") bodily pleasures. Man chooses to rein in his unruly sexual urges. Thus, the virtue of continence resides in the will.

Continence is akin to *temperance* since both concern pleasures of touch, but they are two distinct notions. The subject of the former is the will, whereas that of the latter is the sense appetite. Continence is meant to resist an intense venereal desire; temperance is a tool to moderate sensual pleasures. Continence may be likened to a person who fortifies his or her house to withstand a powerful hurricane, while temperance is a person who builds a windmill to channel the wind for good use (that is, generate electricity).[60]

However, in his *Nicomachean Ethics* Aristotle says that continence is a kind of imperfect virtue or a conditional virtue at best, for it lacks the tranquility and promptness of a true virtue.[61] In a sense, the truly chaste individuals do not have to struggle to do good and resist the seductions of the flesh.[62] They live chastity and purity proactively; there is order in their thoughts, feelings, desires, and conduct at all times. They "have it all together" with moral integrity and emotional maturity, and are the master rather than slave of their passions.

Incontinence[63]

The term *incontinence* is often used in the medical sense—loss of bladder control that results in urine leakage. Here we consider incontinence as a vice by which a person is overcome by the concupiscence of the flesh. Our passions can be strong, yet they are not irresistible. Otherwise, if we could not do anything about our wild tendencies, incontinence would not be a moral issue. Aristotle traces this vice to a combination of weakness and impetuosity. It is mainly a spiritual failure, a neglect in putting up a strong enough fight against wayward desires.

Incontinence is evil in so far as it deviates from reason and plunges into shameful delights. The greater the will or consent, the more wicked the act. Though we can speak of incontinence in a relative sense (excessive craving for food, riches, honor, and so on) strictly speaking this vice refers to venereal pleasures. Hence, we can speak of "incontinence of lust" or the more familiar term, *wantonness*. In Dante's *Inferno*, incontinence is a sin punished in the second through fifth circles. Although it is the lightest of the deadly sins, incontinence of lust would open the gate to deeper layers of hell.

2. Humility[64]

Humility is the virtue that moderates our desire for self-excellence. It is a potential part of temperance, a form of modesty. Acknowledging one's own limitations is the mark of a truly humble person. Humble individuals do not overrate themselves or magnify their achievements. A humble person is *humo acclinis* (literally bent to the ground, inclined to the lowest place). This disposition may come in two ways: by extrinsic principle—when humbled, put down, or belittled by other people—or by intrinsic principle—when, aware of personal failings, one abases him- or herself.

Humility comes next to the theological virtues of faith, hope, and charity, and the cardinal virtue of justice. But it is a foundational virtue, for it is the first step of every conversion. Our sins are pardoned only if we are humble. Humility provides, as it were, "an untrammeled access to spiritual and divine goods."[65] After all, "God opposes the proud, but gives grace to the humble" (Jas 4:6).

In a highly competitive world where people put their best foot forward and walk with head high in a frenetic rat race to the top, humility seems to be countercultural. Success belongs to those who speak their mind, push their way through, and fight for their rights. In a dog-eat-dog environment, one's career or business prospers only if he or she is assertive enough. Being meek and humble looks suited to the weakling and pushover, a trait that will not help anybody go far. Or so it seems.

But humility is actually a quality of dynamic leaders. In a bestseller entitled *Good to Great*, Jim Collins proves that behind the success of excellent companies and organizations, we find able and humble bosses. Normally they

> *didn't* talk about themselves. . . . They'd talk about the company and the contributions of other executives. . . . When

pressed to talk about themselves, they'd say things like, "I hope I'm not sounding like a big shot." Or . . . , "I don't think I can take much credit. We were blessed with marvelous people." Or, "There are plenty of people in this company who could do my job better than I do."[66]

Technically, humility perfects hope, particularly hope in ourselves, for it tempers the mind from seeking what is beyond its capacity. It is not bad to desire great things, for as long as that quest is reasonable. To be more precise, it is all right to aspire for that which surpasses our powers if we trust in God's help, especially since the more we rely on the Almighty, the more he exalts us.

Personal limitations serve as the gauge in moderating one's hope in oneself. If we are secure in the knowledge of our gifts and talents, which ultimately are heaven-sent, we will have little trouble accepting our limits.[67] This humble disposition is shown in one's attitude, conduct, and lifestyle.

It may be harder to find more signs of humility than pride in people in general. But you know when humble persons are present, for they abhor being in the spotlight, listen to you attentively, make apologies, laugh at their own mistakes, welcome contrary opinions, obey their superiors, say thank you, and sit in the back row. Need we say more? Humble individuals do not envy others; they are content with what they have. They seek help and advice; they do not pretend to know everything. They are patient when things do not turn out well, for they are detached from their plans. They do not compare themselves with others but appreciate their good qualities.

The great mathematician-physicist Albert Einstein felt uneasy with praise. "There are plenty of the well-endowed, thank God," he said.

It strikes me as unfair, and even bad taste, to select a few of them for boundless admiration, attributing superhuman powers of mind and character to them. This has been my fate, and the contrast between the popular estimate of my powers and achievements and the reality is simply grotesque.[68]

The humble person tends to the lowest place, but he or she is not obsequious, which is false self-abasement, a form of pride disguised as humility.[69] You know when a person devalues him- or herself or exaggerates one's defects purposely to appear humble. It is a subtle way to draw attention. Pretension is one of the many faces of egoism.

True humility is an inward movement of the soul based on truth and justice. Truth, because it leads us to know ourselves as we are. Justice, because it leads us to act accordingly. Being humble is not about self-disparagement or trampling on our self-esteem. Aquinas says that if a person shuns honor to the point of neglecting to do what deserves honor, he or she is blameworthy. Humble people do not claim to possess what they do not have, nor deny what they do have. "You are the light of the world. . . . Nor do men light a lamp and put it under a bushel, but on a stand, and it gives light to all in the house" (Mt 5:14–15).

St. Paul encourages us to be lowly, saying, "[I]n humility count others better than yourselves" (Phil 2:3). So then, are we supposed to curtsy and kowtow to other people? Aquinas gives a qualified answer full of wisdom. The humble person does not bow to all other people as though they were superior to him or her in all respects. It is not exactly a good idea to salute people who have glaring defects or give a bad example. But since anything excellent comes from God,[70] we do well to appreciate the good qualities of other people. We applaud a superb pianist, honor rescue workers, extol a true leader, commend our hairstylist, and thank our beloved parents—for all the good that they do in their own ways. These are gestures of humility.

The point of reference in humility is God, both for us and for others. Every good thing we have is a gift from on high. "What have you that you did not receive? If then you received it, why do you boast as if it were not a gift?" (1 Cor 4:7). Generally, humble individuals are unimpressionable people. They are not affected much by "what others say." Criticize them and they will take it well. Praise them and they will deflect it. For they do not go around trying to please people, but only God.

Pride[71]

Excellence is one of the intelligible goods that people naturally seek. We have the instinct to do things well, be superior, stand out, achieve, and excel. There is nothing wrong with that. But this natural urge tends to be excessive. People can overestimate their ability and wish to appear more than what they really are. Reason, however, requires that we tend to what is only proportionate to our abilities. Humility is the virtue that tempers our disordered desire for excellence and keeps it within reasonable bounds.

Pride (*superbia*) is the first of the capital vices. It implies an inflated sense of self-worth. All sins, all moral disorders stem from pride. Two elements are present in every sin: turning away from God (aversion from immutable good) and turning toward creatures (conversion to ephemeral good). The critical part of sin is aversion and it is most pronounced in pride. In other areas like sexuality and work, people may offend God through ignorance or weakness, but they will rectify the situation if they are humble. The proud do not own up to their mistakes and refuse to be subject to God.[72]

What humility affirms and preserves, pride denies and contradicts: the creaturely status of the person.[73] Before it is shown
in outward behavior, pride is bred in the mind, will, and heart.
The proud feel uneasy with their defects; they cannot accept
their limitations. That is why pride in its worst form is the rejec-
tion of God: because humility first of all is acknowledging our
subjection to him.[74] Proud individuals are myopic, as it were,
since they have a distorted vision of reality. Or worse, they are
blind, losing the ability to perceive the truth altogether.

Samuel Dresner, an American Jewish scholar, activist, and
author (1923–2000) said that the greatest consequence of
arrogance, and ultimately its most disastrous effect, is spiritual
blindness:

> When our own ego is the constant center of all our concern,
> decisions and actions, and when our own selves are the shin-
> ing hub in which are set the numberless spokes of life, around
> which all our thoughts, feelings and encounters revolve in
> a never changing whirl of self-centeredness, then we have
> blinders over our spiritual eyes.[75]

Pride is a disordered appetite and so it resides in the will. The
proud person is under pressure, makes futile sacrifices, and is full
of delusions of grandeur. Egoism creates a false sense of self-reliance that leads a person to foolishly deny indebtedness to God.
He or she also does things to be noticed, claims all the credits
and throws the blame on others. Proud individuals get mad when
opposed, sad when ignored, and happy when praised. They tend
to be arrogant, boastful, and touchy. Almost by instinct, they
interrupt others when they talk, drop hints of self-praise, make
up stories, resent the success of others, hide their deficiencies, and
look down on those who have less.

The person who wishes to appear more than he or she
is, and thus wants to be preferred to others, is almost always

someone who was inadequately affirmed as a child. His or her prideful manners betray personal insecurities.

> When pride takes hold of a soul, it is no surprise to find it bringing along with it a whole string of other vices: greed, self-indulgence, envy, injustice. The proud man is always vainly striving to dethrone God . . . so as to make room for himself and his ever cruel ways. . . . Pride is the worst sin of all, and the most ridiculous.[76]

One way to overcome pride is to think that from birth to death we live in a state of constant dependence. Yes, we cannot do it all alone, we need others, we count on the help of so many people: parents, teachers, pastors, friends, colleagues, government, and the like. We should thus be grateful for all the benefits we receive, in a spirit of justice and humility. Naturally, our most radical dependence and foremost duty of gratitude is toward God, for to him we owe all that we are and all that we have. "[W]hoever exalts himself will be humbled, and whoever humbles himself will be exalted" (Mt 23:12).

3. Meekness[77]

Meekness is the virtue that restrains the rush of anger. An annexed virtue or potential part of temperance, meekness mitigates the passion of anger in accord with right reason, curbing especially its tendency to vengeance. We resent and fire back at anything or anyone who hurts us. Fair enough! People naturally want to avenge the injuries they suffer. But anger must be moderated. By suppressing fierce anger, meekness prevents us from losing self-control and committing evil.

Meekness is not to be confused with weakness. They may sound alike, but they are quite opposite in meaning. To be meek is to possess oneself, to be in control of one's emotions.

If the hot-tempered person is unable to bridle his or her pro-pensity to flare up, the meek person is able to rein in his or her irascible appetite. Thus, a meek person is not weak but has inner strength; not a slave, but the master of one's passions. To be gentle is not to look harmless and pale-faced, much less to be soft in character. The virtue of meekness teaches us to be mild-mannered and be angry—when we have to—in the proper way.

Recall the times that bad temper spoiled our day and hurt our relationships. Blame it on hormonal imbalance, work pres-sures, or choleric temperament. But much of it is rooted in pride. Self-love makes us think we are always right, while others are always wrong. Plus, today's culture of rugged individualism sub-tly fosters rudeness and discourtesy. "That's the way I am! I say what I feel and do what I want!" People expect us to fight back and get even—tit for tat. If we do not, society tags our meekness as timidity and cowardice.

None of us is perfect; we all have defects. It pays to be under-standing with those who live and work with us (Col 3:13). "Cool head and warm heart, not hot head and cold heart," as the saying goes. Whoever is meek is not given to tantrums and flare-ups. A meek person's reactions are moderate, words mea-sured, tone calm, decisions pondered. *Meekness* in the Sacred Scriptures denotes controlled strength. It is one of the fruits of the Holy Spirit (see Gal 5:22–23), and we see it in people who are serene, composed, equable, mellow, patient, level-headed, and even-tempered. "A soft answer turns away wrath, but a harsh word stirs up anger" (Prv 15:1).

"[L]earn from me; for I am gentle and lowly in heart" (Mt 11:29). Jesus is our model of meekness and humility. The French theologian Adolphe Tanquerey (1854–1932) pointed to this virtue as the way to overcome irritability, bear with our neighbor in spite of his or her flaws, and treat others with charity.

Meekness resides chiefly in the will and emotions, inclining us to be gentle and serene. The virtue does not always come spontaneously, but is acquired with effort.[78]

Wrath[79]

Opposed to meekness is the vice of *wrath*. Anger is a passion of the sensitive appetite. The term *irascible power* derives its name precisely from the Latin *ira*—anger. Anger has many faces: bile, ill-will, rancor, or bitterness. People who are irritable are quick-tempered and choleric.

As a passion, anger is not essentially evil. There are situations in which anger is the right way to react. We naturally get mad, for example, if a street beggar is ridiculed by some rowdy youth, or if we catch someone trying to swindle us, or if a senseless terrorist attack kills innocent civilians. There is such a thing as just anger, holy ire, or lawful indignation. The Letter to the Ephesians says, "Be angry but do not sin" (Eph 4:26). Jesus was enraged seeing the temple treated like a bazaar, so he drove out the merchants, scattered the coins, and overturned the tables (see Mt 21:12–17; Mk 11:15–19; Lk 19:45–48). Always carping and suspicious, the Pharisees watched our Lord to see if he would cure on the Sabbath. So Jesus looked around at them with anger—*circumspiciens eos cum ira*—due to their hardened hearts (see Mk 3:5).

But although a person can be justifiably inflamed, anger can also affect reason in the wrong way. People can overreact, fly into rage, or freak out. You have probably witnessed a scene of road rage, physical attack, verbal outburst, or domestic abuse. An angry person can go overboard, strike back disproportionately, and show murderous impulses. The disorder may be fanned by a combination of what Aristotle calls anger as *choler* (quick-tempered), *sullen* (nursing injuries), and *astern* (desire to revenge).[80] This is what happens when we dwell on our perceived hurts, refuse to forgive the offender, and harbor deep grudges.

Wrath is one of the seven capital sins, for it gives rise to other moral disorders, like the headwater of rivers and streams. Wrath unleashes multiple evils worse than itself, such as quarrelling, cursing, or even murder. The vice of wrath has a blinding effect, for it breaks all bounds and disrupts the order of reason. Man's free judgment of the truth is hindered by the impetus of fury. In a sense, we are out of ourselves if we are enraged. We cannot think straight. The spirit is bitter, the will is violent, the mind is clouded, and the heart is poisoned. We become deaf to the language of truth and love.[81]

The virtue of meekness, in contrast, restores balance and disposes a person to perceive things objectively and act out of charity. In his meditations on the eight Beatitudes, author Jacques Philippe wrote that the practice of patience, the habit of prayer, and the effort to amend our ways would clothe us in meekness and smother, in a way, all traces of hardness and bitterness in our heart. Whatever drives us mad is just temporary, but meekness fills us with inner peace.[82]

If wrath is an excess anger, the opposite extreme is also possible, as when a person is never upset and vexed when he or she should be. This person is insensible by defect, failing to resent evil and use the lawful anger necessary to protect the good. It is certainly better to be fiery when standing up for our ideals and defending good values than to be passive and indifferent about them. Take note that meekness is not the absence of wrath, but its regulation by reason, in the same way that chastity is not the absence of sensuality, but its moderation. Incapacity to be angry at all is a fault and vice, says the Angelic Doctor.[83] Absence of emotion is not a sign of true humanity.

4. Clemency[84]

Clemency is moderation of anger when one exacts retribution or imposes punishment. Since it bridles the passion of a sensitive appetite according to reason, clemency is a potential part of temperance. The virtue denotes a certain sweetness of the soul that leads us to lessen punitive measures, taking into account the pain that might be suffered by the offender. Is the trait of being clement the same as being meek? There is a fine distinction. Aquinas explains that clemency moderates external punishment, while meekness moderates the passion of anger.

As mentioned above, we can be mad but in a tempered way. When we suffer injustice, we have the right to demand recompense. But the restitution should not be disproportionate. If an SUV dents your car, you expect the driver to apologize and pay for the repair. You do well to require compensation, but not an exorbitant amount. Just because you're upset and aggrieved, it is not fair to claim twenty thousand dollars for its repair. Similarly, if you are the school principal and have a faculty member who is tardy for the third time, you may lower his or her performance mark but not fire the person. The virtue of clemency is the way to restore justice without falling into excess. Persons of authority like parents, executives, and judges may have to penalize, but should always do so with clemency.[85]

Cruelty and Leniency[86]

Opposed to clemency are, on the one hand *cruelty* (Latin *cruditas* or rawness), which leads a person to inflict an excessive penalty, and on the other hand *leniency*, which is an unreasonable mitigation of punishment. Aquinas states that a clement person may be licitly *severe* if he remains inflexible in meting out punishment demanded by reason.

Parenting, in particular, is an art that calls for a healthy balance of discipline and affection, severity and tenderness. Over the last century society has seen a radical change from the strict, regimented, child-spanking generations to the more permissive ones who believe in "positive discipline" where children can "be who they are." Theories abound as to the most effective method of child-rearing. But from the moral point of view, the proper approach is a clement exercise of parental authority, neither too harsh nor too lax, neither cruel nor lenient.

"[W]hat son is there whom his father does not discipline?" (Heb 12:7). But St. Paul also reminds parents to be reasonable, saying, "Fathers, do not provoke your children to anger, but bring them up in the discipline and instruction of the Lord" (Eph 6:4).

By excess of clemency, lenient authorities harm justice. This vice is a disservice to the erring persons who are thus deprived of the benefits of correction. A judge, dean, or parent who is lenient tend to be passive, neglectful, and indifferent. Students tend to slack off if the professor is indulgent. Criminals are emboldened if the justice system has loopholes. Employees end up corrupt if the boss is tolerant of malpractice. And kids are deformed if Mom and Dad set no rules on eating habits, internet access, sleeping patterns, gadget use, house chores, and the like.

By lack of clemency, *cruel* authorities can also harm justice. The vice of *cruelty* implies a certain hardness of heart that inclines a person to punish more than what is necessary or impose a disproportionate sanction. The cruel person is merciless, harsh, and abusive.

Cruelty can degenerate into *brutality* or *savagery*, which refers to the infliction of punishment on the innocent. A brutal or savage act is not motivated by a sense of justice but by the sheer "pleasure" of seeing others suffer or tortured. Guilt and innocence are irrelevant. Terrorists fit this description, for they sow violence and inflict harm indiscriminately. They are bereft of human feeling and sensibility.

5. Modesty[87]

Modesty is a potential part of temperance, a virtue that is ordered to chastity and protects the intimate center of the person. It means refusing to unveil what should remain hidden. Modesty guides how we look at others and behave toward them in conformity with the dignity of persons.[88] It regulates our external deportment, inclining us to observe what is proper in conduct, movement, speech, posture, dress, and entertainment.[89] A modest person is discreet, silent, and reserved, especially when there is evident risk of unhealthy curiosity.

Strictly, if *temperance* moderates what is hardest to control (palate and genitalia), *modesty* regulates the less powerful urges of the person which are thus less difficult to manage. A person ought to practice modesty and propriety in one's deportment, clothing, learning, and recreation.

a. Decorum[90]

Bodily movement is an index of the soul. The way a person acts, moves, looks, speaks, and carries oneself reflects his or her inner disposition. Our external conduct must be regulated by the virtue of modesty as decorum (*honestas*) so that it is well-ordered, fitting, and beautiful. Otherwise, we end up acting in a way that is disgraceful and unbecoming to persons, which is ultimately animal lust.

Popular wisdom says that anything in excess is bad. Temperance governs all human desires, passions, and activities. Decorum is all about good manners and social graces, the ability to fit into polite society, blend with others, and behave with etiquette. Our gestures, appearance, reaction, tone of voice, choice of words, gaze and gait, and so forth can cross the boundary of what is proper and acceptable. Modesty shuns boisterous laughter, airs of pedantry, crashing a party, flirtatious remarks, affected poise, scatological humor, and other unseemly behaviors.

Modest conduct is prudent behavior. There is affability and refinement. At home, at work, in the bus, church, airport, or restaurant, we try to get along with people. Our dignified comportment builds healthy relationships. We do not interrupt others when they talk, and we offer our seat to the elderly, silence our phone in a meeting, wait for our turn in line, and so forth. Our conversations are not frivolous, but carry a certain dignity (*gravitas*). Quite naturally we show thoughtfulness and respect for others. Thanks to the virtue of modesty, we have a pleasant aspect, gentle demeanor, mature character, and well-balanced personality.

b. Apparel[91]

Clothing is of particular interest. Civilized people are expected to be decent and discreet. Reason demands that we dress up and cover our bodies. Shirts and shorts are neutral and amoral, but men and women are not. The way people wear clothing matters. A person can be immodest either because he or she is skimpily clad, too picky about one's attire, or dresses up in utter disregard of social norms. Modesty also requires that we do not go around in dirty and slovenly clothing.

Over half a century ago, Pius XII addressed the leading figures of the fashion world and encouraged them to imbue their work with a Christian spirit. His words resonate to this day. Fashion, the Holy Father said, is the confluence of various psychological and moral factors such as the love of beauty, the thirst for novelty, the affirmation of personality, and the distaste for monotony; it is also an expression of luxury, ambition, and vanity. Fashion is elegance, but characterized by a constant change, driven by a certain anxiety to overcome the past, fostered by the frenetic rhythm of the contemporary times. It has a tremendous power to gratify the senses and fantasy.[92]

Everyone—including boys and men—should live modesty in apparel, but especially women, for the exposition of the female body tends to arouse concupiscence more easily. Girls and ladies can wear outfit for reasons of frivolity, vanity, or coquetry.[93] The world, of course, does not lack decent and respectable women who defy sexy fashion trends to don modest yet elegant attire. Still, these days the city streets are littered with walking mannequins: miniskirts, tight-fit jeans, see-through dresses, low waistlines, undersized blouses, plunging necklines, and spaghetti straps. Note, however, that a woman or man whose body is well covered is not necessarily modest for that reason; she or he may put on turtlenecks and cardigans due to chilly winter temperatures. Virtue is doing what is morally good, not what is practical.

Modesty

> protests . . . against the voyeuristic explorations of the human body . . . or against the solicitations of certain media that go too far in the exhibition of intimate things. Modesty inspires a way of life which makes it possible to resist the allurements of fashion and the pressures of prevailing ideologies.[94]

Naturally, customs vary across different cultures. Topless women are normal in some African tribes, but are considered offensive in the West. Context is also important. It is perfectly fine for a woman or a man to wear a swimsuit at the beach, but not in the office. What is fashionable for a teen may be grotesque for an older woman. In theory, nudity may be a licit subject of artwork, but this often raises practical moral problems. Modesty cannot be quantified nor seen as black and white. The true measure of modesty is the rule of reason. That said, modesty exists everywhere as an intuition of the spiritual dignity proper to the human person, born of and nourished by the awareness that he or she is not an object (of pleasure) but a subject (of dignity).[95]

In Western societies, where freedom and individualism are highly prized, many people break traditional social customs and taboos in clothing and lifestyles. The lax, vulgar, popular, and casual tend to undermine timeless values. Not to mention the proliferation of social media, where people upload snapshots of what they do in the kitchen or bedroom in ways that are largely unrestricted, unfiltered, unsavory, and immodest.

c. Studiousness[96]

Temperance moderates not just the sensitive appetites like the desire to eat, drink, and have sex, but also the intellectual appetites like the desire to know. A potential part of temperance, *studiousness* is the virtue that moderates our natural inclination to possess knowledge. It serves as a restraint to a person's tendency to seek and learn excessively or inordinately. But this same studiousness is also a spur to study, a keenness of interest in knowing the truth of things."

"All men by nature desire to know," says Aristotle in the first line of his *Metaphysics*. We have the innate tendency to learn, discover, explore, search, know, and seek answers. Knowledge of the truth is an intelligible human good. It is the basis of the basic human right to education. Man's quest for knowledge is the origin of schools, colleges, and universities. Libraries and laboratories exist for that reason. Every day millions of people use search engines and web browsers to check the weather forecast, read world news, or look up the meaning of a word.

But as in all other human activities, intellectual pursuits can be tainted by disorder. *Studiositas* can degenerate into *curiositas*, which is intemperance in learning. Aquinas explains how this defect comes about. Thus, a person a) may seek knowledge to take pride in it, b) may try to know how to carry out something immoral, c) may be learning useless things when he or she should know only what is needed, d) may obtain knowledge from wrong sources, e) may strive to study realities without any reference to God, and f) may foolishly try to master what is beyond his or her capacity.[97]

This sounds complex but it is not really. If you are checking the real-time NFL scores, standings, and results on your iPhone when you're supposed to be listening to an ongoing Mass homily, that's curiosity. So also, if you read much about the San Andreas Fault or the D-Day Normandy landings just to outwit others, or you delve into the issue of human trafficking of sex slaves with an unhealthy motive, that's curiosity. We can also be too nosy about other people's affairs that are really none of our business. And so on and so forth.

It is a virtue to be *studious*. We do well to desire to know what is true, good, and beneficial for ourselves and for others. The student who studies and prepares well for an exam deserves credit. Yet our desire to be knowledgeable applies not just to immediate and practical problems we need to solve, such as which documents are needed for passport renewal or which bibliographical sources should be cited in an essay, but also to higher values and more lofty knowledge for personal fulfillment and service to society.

But temperance has to step in when we fall into *curiosity*. The unrestrained desire to know is rooted in the concupiscence of the eyes. We are gifted with vision so we can perceive reality. Obviously the sense of sight is in itself good. But disorder is introduced by concupiscence when we seek the pleasure of seeing, when we watch, stare, look, and ogle simply because we enjoy doing so. It is seeing not in order to attain knowledge but to wallow in the world.[98] Curiosity is a sign of a restless mind, attached heart, and worldly spirit.

Our competitive society pushes us to be up-to-date, catch the latest news, and be aware of trends. So we frequently surf the internet, open newspapers, and read magazines to be informed. But it is not about absorbing a plethora of data. It is wise to choose what to read and process the information. For one, it is physically impossible to read everything. For another, a lot of things written are useless. Modesty regulates our hunger to know and helps focus on learning what truly matters and on doing it the right way.

d. Recreation (Eutrapelia)[99]

One important aspect of life is rest and recreation. We all need to unwind, relax, play sports, or engage in some other diversions, especially after a tiring work week. A person grows weary and is liable to mental and physical fatigue. Rest does not just mean catching some sleep or slouching on the sofa to watch movies. The soul generally finds an easing of tensions in lighter activities like sports or other forms of entertainment. In Aristotle's *Nicomachean Ethics*, the virtue of *eutrapelia* means the habit of a pleasant and cheerful turn of mind, shown in our attitudes, words, and actions.[100]

But there are limits to observe. Play becomes a disorder if it is a) discourteous, scandalous, injurious, obscene, or insolent, or b) inordinate due to circumstances like place and time. The first type is always wrong, for no one in his or her right mind would watch pornography or kick others as a form of pastime.

The second type depends on whether it disobeys God's laws or violates certain Church precepts. Going on a mountain hike or a fishing expedition is a restful weekend escapade. But if a Catholic forgoes Sunday Mass for this reason, what is virtuous becomes a vice, and recreation becomes intemperance.

In our high-tech generation, not only kids but also many adults are hooked online for hours on end. Gadgets limit the face-to-face interaction of family members. They eat meals facing a screen. People watch videos or play computer games until the early hours of the morning. Not to mention eye strain, physical fatigue, poor sleep patterns, and bad posture. This is a classic form of intemperance in rest and entertainment.

It is good to have fun. Even more, it is necessary to rest. We just have to remember the proper measure: not too little, nor too much, nor the wrong kind of diversion. While some people spend too much time in the gym, others are too engrossed in work. The former live a rather lax and carefree lifestyle, while the latter follow a dull, mirthless, and bland routine. Temperance, as regards diversion, means a healthy work-life balance.

6. Virginity[101]

We speak of a virgin forest (old-growth forest), virgin raw material (not recycled), a virgin beach (pristine shores), extra virgin olive oil (pure and cold-pressed), and so on. They all convey the same idea of being untouched, undefiled, or unsullied.

Similarly, *virginity* (from *viror*, freshness) is that virtue whose material element is the integrity of the flesh and whose formal element is the desire to abstain from all venereal pleasures for God's sake. It is this motive that makes virginity a moral virtue, affirms Aquinas. Giving up sex and marriage alone does not make anybody virtuous; he or she may do it for fear of disease and to avoid family responsibilities. Virginity is a choice that implies total sexual integrity, consecrating oneself, both body and soul, in honor of the Creator.

Virginity has a special excellence. Keeping oneself free from any sexual activity is more perfect than just avoiding inordinate sexual pleasures. Virginal continence deserves greater praise than marital continence. Virginity is related to chastity in the same way that magnificence is related to liberality. It is superior to married life for the following reasons: the divine good takes precedence over any human good, spiritual needs are preferrable to bodily needs, and contemplative life (dedication to God) is better than active life (concerns of the world). The Blessed Mother is a virgin, or rather the *Virgin* par excellence, and Jesus himself was celibate. St. Paul also attested to the greater excellence of virginity. However, he mentioned it by way of counsel, not an imposition, because at the end of the day, "each has his own special gift from God, one of one kind and one of another" (1 Cor 7:6–8).

The words of St. Paul puts things in perspective. While, *objectively*, virginity is on a higher plane than marriage, *subjectively*, each person has a specific vocation. God has a plan for each one of us and we ought to discern and follow that path. If your calling is to form a family and work in the middle of the world, it is not a good idea to embrace virginity or celibacy. Needless to say, marriage is not a sin and the great majority of men and women are called to conjugal life. Marriage is a great sacrament (*sacramentum magnum*, see Eph 5:32) and a path to sanctity for couples who reflect the mystery of Christ's loving union with his Bride, the Church.[102]

St. Catherine of Genoa (1447–1510), who was married, did not like the contrasting of the married and virginal persons (*in concreto*) as beings of different value, instead of the contrasting (*in abstracto*) of marriage and virginity per se.[103] She definitely had a point. We can be sure that there are ordinary folks in the markets, factories, schools, laboratories, or homes who are holier than cloistered religious. The ultimate basis of holiness is not our chosen state in life, but how we love God and live fraternal charity. Regardless of our personal vocation, we all have the capacity to be good and the means to attain sanctity.

7. Parsimony and Simplicity[104]

So far, we have seen temperance as moderation in food, drink, sex, anger, bearing, apparel, self-esteem, learning, punishment, and recreation. There is one more area where we ought to practice self-control—the use of material goods. *Parsimony* is the virtue by which a person is content with what he has, not striving for too many possessions. Related to this is the virtue of *simplicity*, whereby we refrain from being too fussy and choosy about material things.

Aquinas treats greed as a vice opposed to the virtue of liberality. But greed also goes against temperance, for it implies disordered attachment to earthly riches. Otherwise known as *covetousness, greed* inclines a person to amass excessive wealth and resort to unjust ways (for example, stealing) of acquiring riches. However, greed is not always externalized. It can be nurtured in one's heart by someone who loves money and takes too much pleasure in wealth.[105] The tenth commandment forbids avarice and envy: "You shall not covet . . . anything that is your neighbor's" (Ex 20:17).

We do not despise created goods. A person needs material things to live with dignity, in keeping with his or her life conditions. We exercise dominion and stewardship over the earth (see Gn 1:26–30). It is perfectly all right to enjoy its fruits. Property ownership is a basic human right. If you look around, everything that you see ultimately comes from nature, whether it is a rocking chair, a mobile phone, sliced bread, red wine, a winter coat, bond paper, the automobile, you name it. *Homo laborans* (working man) may have transformed the raw materials into fine, ready-to-use products, but every single item bears the imprint of the Creator, and everything he makes is radically good (Gn 1:31).

However, we must not forget the instrumental nature of things. Dominion degenerates into slavery when a person falls into greed. It is a form of the concupiscence of the eyes that consists in the disordered attachment to earthly goods. The evil lies in one's excesses, by wishing to acquire and keep riches immoderately. Greed is a capital vice, since the love of money (which is a form of idolatry) leads to all sorts of moral disorders called daughters of avarice: treachery (betrayal of people), fraud (insincerity in deeds), falsehood (deception in words), perjury (false oath), restlessness (excessive anxiety and care, never being satisfied), violence (tendency to use force), and insensibility to mercy (a hardened heart that is indisposed to help the needy).[106]

Some guidance might help illustrate these points. Is there integrity in our business dealings? Do we purchase items out of sheer impulse? Is our lifestyle in accord with our means? Do we fancy acquiring this and that? Can we forgo something that we like? Do we keep track of our expenses? Are there useless items stockpiled in our closet? Are we envious of those who are better off? The Greek philosopher Socrates apparently walked down the central market of Athens and gruffly harrumphed: "Oh, how many things I don't need!"

Temperance means acknowledging that we are the steward of the things we possess, not their absolute owner. A good antidote to greed is a spirit of detachment, shown in living a simple and sober life, as well as generosity, especially toward the needy. American Catholic social activist Dorothy Day (1897–1980) said that if you have two coats, one of them belongs to the poor.

"Blessed are the poor in spirit, for theirs is the kingdom of heaven" (Mt 5:3). A great paradox laid down by Jesus in the Beatitudes is poverty in spirit: to be rich in God's eyes, one has to be detached from material things. This Christian ideal seems unpopular in a world gripped by the frenzy to own a status symbol and where one's net worth is the gauge of success. But true happiness cannot be found in wealth because the more things we accumulate, the more we realize their insufficiency. Stories abound of very affluent people who are sad and depressed. Money does not bring happiness: in fact, it is often a source of spiritual bankruptcy. What is important is being, becoming better; not having, possessing more.

Temperance and detachment penetrate the interior of the human person in order to uproot avarice and broaden the horizons of the intellect and the will, in such a way that the soul is attuned to God and shows deeds of love. When we open ourselves to the transcendent, we experience our capacity for the infinite that is proper to every human heart.[107]

Christian Temperance

Everything that we have said so far refers mostly to the human virtue of temperance, the habit of moderation and self-control that we can acquire by dint of effort to tame our sensual desires and fight the seductions of the flesh. Guided by reason, we try to avoid excesses and develop self-mastery.

Acquired temperance is essential, but it does not tell the whole story. For the love of God, someone might eat just a morsel of buttered toast when it is perfectly alright (that is reasonable) to have a bacon and egg sandwich. It is not bad to watch a Broadway musical or drink gin and tonic, but a person may give these up for a higher motive. These acts can be explained by the *supernatural virtue of temperance* by which a Christian behaves under the light of faith, not merely by the rule of reason.

Supernatural temperance or *Christian temperance* is not acquired by one's effort but infused by God and so belongs to the order of grace. It gives the person a radical capacity to act on a higher plane, yet one built on his or her natural dispositions. With the infused virtue, we do not only strive to be humanly fulfilled, but to be holy. Pious people often perform little acts of self-denial like taking a cold shower or skipping dessert. They do these not for health reasons but because of their supernatural outlook. Giving up meat on a Friday makes no sense for a nonbeliever, but for a Christian it is a means of sanctification.

Grace does not destroy or substitute for nature. The infused virtue does not render human effort superfluous; it presupposes and perfects it. Someone with a gentle character is better inclined toward Christian meekness. Holy purity is easier to practice if we are naturally chaste. We keep on the fight to moderate our desire for self-excellence, knowledge, possessions, or recreation even if we get divine help, even if God pours a torrent of graces into our soul. In fact, a person of faith goes the extra mile to abstain from legitimate pleasures.

The acquired virtue of temperance has something provisional and imperfect in it. The Christian vision of life shows that a person can only attain his or her fullest human potential through union with God and imitation of Jesus Christ. Ultimate perfection is beyond our reach in this world, especially since the reality of sin inclines us to evil. Experience attests to the fact that we are morally fragile. On the whole, the practice of virtues is hard, but temperance is especially difficult because of our powerful urges, mood swings, and ingrained habits. Therefore, we need to cooperate with divine grace so that we are wholly transformed.[108]

One effective method to foster temperance is Christian mortification (literally, "putting the flesh to death"), a form of spiritual discipline linked to Christ's supreme sacrifice on the Cross. By making acts of self-denial, we purify our soul, atone for our sins, defeat temptations, chastise our impulses, and develop saintly dispositions. Holiness has a price tag: renunciation and ascetical battle.

The person's carnal desires are like a twisted wire that can only be straightened by twisting it the opposite way.[109] That is the very idea of self-denial. We give up a piece of cake, cast no glance, sit well and erect, bite our tongue, wake up on the dot, finish our task, and offer up the pain—because we want to overcome the lust of the flesh and develop self-dominion. What our body craves, what we feel like doing, is often pure caprice. So it helps to learn to say no to ourselves in some way. These acts of mortification ensure that our life is governed by reason illumined by faith, not by passions full of worldliness.

It is easy to let ourselves be carried away by natural impulses, but this road ends up in sadness and misery, whereas a temperate person is free from all kinds of slavery. "Temperance makes the soul sober, modest, understanding. It fosters a natural sense of reserve which everyone finds attractive because it denotes intelligent self control."[110] "[F]or if you live according to the flesh you will die, but if by the Spirit you put to death the deeds of the body you will live" (Rom 8:13).

SOURCES

Introduction

1. Alasdair MacIntyre, *After Virtue*, 3rd ed. (Indiana: University of Notre Dame Press, 2007), p. 150.

2. Aristotle, *Nicomachean Ethics* 3.2.

3. *Catechism of the Catholic Church*, 2nd ed (Washington, DC: Libreria Editrice Vaticana–United States Conference of Catholic Bishops, 2000), nos. 1803–1804.

4. Julio Dieguez, "Reaching the Entire Person: Role of the Emotions," Opus Dei, September 5, 2018, *https://opusdei.org/en/article/reaching-the-entire-person-role-of-the-emotions-1/*.

5. St. Thomas Aquinas, *Summa Theologica* 2-2.61.3–4.

6. William J. Bennett, ed., *The Book of Virtues: A Treasury of Great Moral Stories* (New York: Simon and Schuster, 1993), p. 14.

7. Chris Hazell, "Q&A: Dr. Angela Knobel's New Book on Aquinas and the Moral Virtues," University of Dallas, accessed February 15, 2022, *https://news.udallas.edu/2021-07-27-Q-A-Dr-Angela-Knobels-New-Book-on-Aquinas-and-the-Moral-Virtues*.

8. Hazell; see also John A. Hardon, SJ, "The Meaning of Virtue in St. Thomas Aquinas," Christendom Media, Christendom College, accessed February 15, 2022, *https://media.christendom.edu/2001/04/the-meaning-of-virtue-in-st-thomas-aquinas/*.

CHAPTER ONE The Virtue of Prudence

1. Allowing for the limit of the metaphor.

2. Man's autonomy is not absolute, nor is a person fully self-sufficient who can do whatever he or she wants. We are dependent on the moral law, and ultimately on God (*Catechism of the Catholic Church*, no. 1740).

3. Gn 1:26–28.

4. Juan Luis Lorda, *The Virtues of Holiness: The Basics of Spiritual Struggle* (New York: Scepter, 2010), p. 49.

5. *Catechism of the Catholic Church*, no. 1731.

6. Jutta Burggraf, *Made for Freedom* (New York: Scepter, 2012), p. 2.

7. Aristotle, 6.5.

8. Aquinas, 2-2.47.2.

9. St. Augustine, *De moribus Ecclesiae*, 1, 15, 25.

10. Bennett, p. 186.

11. Aquinas, 2-2.47.14. Children who are baptized but do not have yet the use of reason have gratuitous prudence by divine infusion. They have prudence as to habit, but not as to act.

12. David Isaacs, *La Educación de las Virtudes Humanas y su Evaluación, Tomo 2* (Pamplona, Spain: Ediciones Universidad de Navarra, 1981), p. 142.

13. Burggraf, p. 18.

14. William Mattison III, *Introducing Moral Theology: True Happiness and the Virtues* (Grand Rapids: Brazos, 2008), p. 111.

15. Aquinas, 2-2.47.7.

16. Josef Pieper, *The Four Cardinal Virtues* (Indiana: University of Notre Dame Press, 1966), pp. 7–8.

17. Celestine Bittle, *Man and Morals* (Milwaukee: Bruce, 1950), p. 255.

18. Aristotle, *Nicomachean Ethics*, 6.5.

19. Pieper, p. 29.

20. Aquinas, 2-2.47.13.

21. Joseph Rickaby, *Four Square, or, The Cardinal Virtues* (New York: Veritatis Splendor, 2012), p. 21.

22. Jacques Maritain, "The Philosophy of Art; Ethics," part 2, chap. 9 in *An Introduction to Philosophy* (Lanham, MD: Rowman & Littlefield, 2005).

23. Aquinas, 2-2.47.3.

24. Aquinas, 1.79.12.

25. Pieper, pp. 10–11.

26. "Synderesis," Oxford Reference, Oxford University Press, accessed January 20, 2022, *https://www.oxfordreference.com/view/10.1093/oi/authority.20110803100547470.*

27. Douglas McManaman, *A Treatise on the Four Cardinal Virtues* (San Bernardino, CA: McManaman, 2013), pp. 7–8.

28. McManaman, p. 8.

29. Pieper, p. 11.

30. Pieper, p. 13.

31. St. Josemaría Escrivá, *Friends of God* (London: Scepter, 1981), no. 79.

32. F. J. Sheed, *Theology and Sanity* (New York: Sheed & Ward, 1946), pp. 157–159.

33. Internet Encyclopedia of Philosophy, s.v. "Thomas Aquinas: Moral Philosophy," by Shawn Floyd, accessed January 20, 2022, *https://iep.utm.edu/aq-moral/*.

34. McManaman, p. 17.

35. Pieper, p. 15.

36. Aquinas, 2-2.49.2; see also Mark O'Keefe, *Virtues Abounding* (Eugene, OR: Cascade, 2019), p. 18 and Richard Regan, *Aquinas: The Cardinal Virtues* (Indianapolis, IN: Hackett, 2005), p. 12.

37. Van Bryan, "Heraclitus (535- 475 BCE)," Classical Wisdom, accessed February 21, 2022, *https://classicalwisdom.com/people/philosophers/heraclitus-535-475-bce/*

38. Aquinas, 2-2.49.3.

39. Escrivá, no. 86.

40. Lorda, p. 52.

41. Pieper, pp. 16–17; see also O'Keefe, p. 17.

42. Christian Crews, Ted Farrington, and Laura Schlehuber, "Understanding Strategic Foresight: The History of Scenario Planning," Viewpoints, Kalypso, March, 2017, *https://kalypso.com/viewpoints/entry/understanding-strategic-foresight-the-history-of-scenario-planning*.

43. Aquinas, 2-2.49.6.

44. Pieper, p. 18.

45. Aquinas, 2-2.49.7.

46. Aquinas, 2-2.30. An action that has foreseen harmful effects inseparable from the good effect is justifiable if the following are true: 1) The nature of the act is itself good, or at least morally neutral; 2) the agent intends the good effect, not the bad effect either as a means to the good or as an end in itself; and 3) the good effect outweighs the bad effect in circumstances sufficiently grave to justify causing the bad effect and the agent exercises due diligence to minimize the harm.

47. The so-called principle of double-effect is discussed in Aquinas, 2-2.64.7.

48. Aquinas, 2-2.49.8.

49. As quoted in "Wisdom in Tough Times from Thomas More," Catholic Insight, June 22, 2021, *https://catholicinsight.com/wisdom-in-tough-times-from-thomas-more/*.

50. The potential parts of a virtue are its derived parts. They differ from the principal virtue but resemble it.

51. Aquinas, 2-2.48.1.

52. Jeff McKay, "Prudent Decision-Making for Leaders," PrudentPedal, Rattle & Pedal, accessed January 20, 2022, *https://www.prudentpedal.com/prudent-decision-making*.

53. McManaman, p. 24.

54. McKay.

55. Aquinas, 2-2.48.1.

56. Steven J. Jensen, "Of Gnome and Gnomes," *American Catholic Philosophical Quarterly* 82, no. 3 (Summer 2008): pp. 411–428, *https://doi.org/10.5840/acpq200882328*.

57. Aquinas, 2-2.51.4; see also McManaman, pp. 24–25.

58. *Gnome* is closely related to *epikeia*, the virtue by which one sets aside the letter of the law (which by nature is imperfect) to follow the demands of justice and the common good. The object of *epikeia* is equity. Aquinas, 2-2.120.1.

59. Isaacs, p. 138.

60. Aquinas, 2-2.53.3–35.

61. McManaman, p. 25.

62. McManaman, pp. 25–26.

63. Aquinas, 2-2.55.1–8.

64. Aquinas, 2-2.55.1; 2-2.47.13.

65. Aquinas, 2-2.55.4.

66. *Code of Canon Law*, no. 1101. Vatican website: *www.vatican.va*.

67. Jonathan Dolhenty, "Part 6: The Virtue of Prudence, Vices Associated with Prudence," Self-Educated American, March 25, 2014, *https://selfeducatedamerican.com/2014/03/25/part-6-the-virtue-of-prudence-vices-associated-with-prudence/*.

68. Aquinas, 2-2.50.1–4.

69. Aquinas, 2-2.47.10–11.

70. Dolhenty. Note that the "technical prudence" or "imperfect prudence" we discussed earlier was in reference to wise decisions made purely from a technical point of view (for example, use of skills in business and ship navigation)

without regard to man's final end. In reality, the moral virtue of prudence applies, and hence, must be observed practically in all human affairs.

71. Pieper, p. 11.

72. Aquinas, 2-2.47.6.

73. Regan, p. 1.

74. Pieper, p. 33.

75. However, the other moral virtues also need prudence in order to carry out their principal act, which is to choose and execute proper conduct. Since the more we do good, the more we are inclined to it, prudence bears fruits in terms of better disposition, giving rise to a symbiotic relationship between rectitude of the end and rectitude of the means.

76. Pieper, p. 33.

77. Pieper, pp. 23–24.

78. Servais Pinckaers, *The Sources of Christian Ethics* (Washington, DC: The Catholic University of America Press, 1955), pp. 454–456.

79. Alasdair MacIntyre, p. 150.

80. McManaman, p. 9.

81. Fr. William P. Saunders, "What Do We Mean by 'Follow Your Conscience'?," Catholic Straight Answers, accessed January 20, 2022, *https://catholic straightanswers.com/what-do-we-mean-by-follow-your-conscience/*.

82. Benedict XVI, Address to the UN General Assembly, New York (April 18, 2008). Vatican website: *www.vatican.va*.

83. St. John Paul II, Encyclical on the Splendor of Truth *Veritatis Splendor* (August 6, 1993), no. 1. Vatican website: *www.vatican.va*.

84. Mattison III, p. 111.

85. *Catechism of the Catholic Church*, no. 1778. This section of the *Catechism* is the basis for the surrounding paragraphs as well.

86. Charles Belmonte, ed., *Faith Seeking Understanding*, vol. 2 (Manila, Philippines: Studium Theologiae Foundation, 2006), p. 45.

87. As quoted in Cardinal George Pell, "On True and False Conscience," Zenit, February 10, 2005, EWTN, *https://www.ewtn.com/catholicism/library/on-true-and-false-conscience-3954*.

88. *Catechism of the Catholic Church*, no. 1778.

89. Although not with absolute certitude, but only in a broad sense.

90. Belmonte, *Faith Seeking Understanding*, vol. 2, p. 48.

91. *Catechism of the Catholic Church*, no. 1790.

92. *Catechism of the Catholic Church*, no. 1791; see also Mattison III, p. 108.

93. St. Pius X, Encyclical on Teaching Christian Doctrine *Acerbo Nimis* (April 15, 1905), no. 5. Vatican website: *www.vatican.va*. Ignorance is called *crass* or *supine* if it is deliberately fostered by someone intent to avoid fulfilling his or her obligation and who instead does what he or she wants.

94. Mary Ann Glendon, "Mary Ann Glendon on Today's University Students, Zenit, April 5, 2004, EWTN, *https://www.ewtn.com/catholicism/library/mary-ann-glendon-on-todays-university-students-10313*.

95. In moral theology, this is referred to as *supererogatory effort* or effort beyond the call of duty.

96. *Catechism of the Catholic Church*, no. 1793; see also Belmonte, *Faith Seeking Understanding*, vol. 2, p. 49.

97. *Catechism of the Catholic Church*, no. 1783.

98. St. John Paul II, *Veritatis Splendor*, no. 60.

99. St. John Paul II, Apostolic Constitution on the Publication of the Catechism of the Catholic Church *Fidei Depositum* (October 11, 1992). Vatican website: *www.vatican.va*.

100. Pius XII, Encyclical Letter *Mystici Corporis* (June 29, 1943), no. 88. Vatican website: *www.vatican.va*.

101. Benedict Baur, *Frequent Confession: Its Place in the Spiritual Life* (Houston: Lumen Christi, 1984), p. 54.

102. C. S. Lewis, *Mere Christianity* (New York: HarperOne, 2001), p. 77.

103. Fr. Andrew Pinsent, *Prudence, Justice, Courage & Temperance* (London: Catholic Truth Society, 2017), pp. 21–23.

104. Pinsent, pp. 18–19.

CHAPTER TWO   The Virtue of Justice

1. St. Augustine, *City of God*, bk. 14, chap. 1, as quoted in *Nicene and Post-Nicene Fathers, First Series*, vol. 2, ed. Philip Schaff, trans. Marcus Dods (Buffalo, NY: Christian Literature, 1887; NewAdvent online version, Kevin Knight), *https://www.newadvent.org/fathers/120114.htm*.

2. Aquinas, 2-2.58.1, as quoted in *The Summa Theologiae of St. Thomas Aquinas*, 2nd ed., trans. Fathers of the English Dominican Province (London: Burns, Oates, and Washbourne, 1920; Kevin Knight, 2017), *https://www.newadvent.org/summa/3058.htm#article1*; see also Romanus Cessario, *The Virtues of the Examined Life* (New York: Continuum, 2002), chap. 5.2, ebook version.

3. McManaman, p. 31.

4. Rafael Burgaleta, *Tratado de las Virtudes Cardinales* (Madrid: Pontificio Instituto de Teología Regina Virginum, 1968), p. 58.

5. Aquinas, 2-2.58.4.

6. See Jean Porter, "Preliminary Considerations," chap. 1 in *Justice as a Virtue: A Thomistic Perspective* (Grand Rapids, MI: William B. Eerdmans, 2016), ebook version.

7. Kevin Timpe and Craig Boyd, *Virtues & Their Vices* (New York: Oxford University Press, 2014), p. 60.

8. Aquinas, 2-2.58.12.

9. Cessario, chap. 5.3, ebook version.

10. Angel Rodríguez Luño, *Chosen in Christ to Be Saints*, vol. 3, *Moral Virtues and Bioethics*, etica & politica, *https://www.eticaepolitica.net/corsodimorale/Chosen_III.pdf*, p. 61.

11. Aquinas, 2-2.58.8.

12. Aquinas, 2-2.79.1; see also Paul J. Glenn, "Modesty as Decorum," A Tour of the Summa, CatholicTheology.info, *http://www.catholictheology.info/summa-theologica/summa-part2B.php?q=192*.

13. Aquinas, 2-2.79.2.

14. Aquinas, 2-2.61.1–4.

15. Aquinas, 2-2.61.3.

16. *Catechism of the Catholic Church*, no. 2411.

17. Aquinas, 2-2.61.2.

18. Burgaleta, p. 89.

19. Aquinas, 2-2.57.1.

20. The notion of *in medio virtus* does not imply mediocrity; rather, it refers to a summit (a peak) between two contrary defects (for example, a brave act is the mean between cowardice and rashness; an act of temperance is the mean between indulgence and insensibility).

21. Aquinas, 2-2.58.10.

22. Aquinas, 2-2.57.1.; see also Regan, p. 31.

23. Pieper, pp. 47–48.

24. Rodríguez Luño, p. 68.

25. Ando Clifford, *Law, Language, and Empire in the Roman Tradition* (Philadelphia: University of Pennsylvania Press, 2011), p. 29; see also Wikipedia, s.v. "Jus gentium," accessed February 11, 2022, *https://en.wikipedia.org/wiki/Jus_gentium*.

26. Aquinas, 2-2.57.3; see also Regan, p. 32, and Enrique Moliné, *The Theological and Moral Virtues*, in Belmonte, p. 150.

27. Cessario, chap. 5.2, ebook version.

28. Moliné, p. 151.

29. Aquinas, 2-2.57.2.

30. Aquinas, 2-2.57.4. There is a hierarchy of relations in which the scope of justice involving husband and wife is greater than that of father and child, and this in turn is greater than that of master and servant.

31. Aquinas, 2-2.57.4.

32. David Gallagher, *Thomas Aquinas on the Perfect Form of Justice*. Unpublished paper delivered at the 40th International Congress on Medieval Studies, Kalamazoo, Michigan, May 7, 2005. David Gallagher is a former philosophy professor at the Catholic University of America. He made available a copy of this unpublished article to the author of this book.

33. Aristotle, 5.19.

34. Gallagher, "Thomas Aquinas and the Perfect Form of Justice."

35. *Catechism of the Catholic Church*, no. 1905.

36. *Catechism of the Catholic Church*, nos. 1908–1909.

37. *Catechism of the Catholic Church*, no. 1910.

38. *Catechism of the Catholic Church*, no. 1911.

39. Aquinas, 1-2.90.4, as quoted in *The Summa Theologiae of St. Thomas Aquinas*, 2nd ed., *https://www.newadvent.org/summa/2090.htm#article4*.

40. *Catechism of the Catholic Church*, nos. 1897–1904.

41. Aquinas, 1-2.96.2.

42. St. John Paul II, Encyclical on the Gospel of Life *Evangelium Vitae* (March 25, 1995), no. 72. Vatican website: *www.vatican.va*.

43. Aquinas, 1-2.93.3.

44. Aquinas, 2-2.59.1–4.

45. Regan, p. 41.

46. O'Keefe, pp. 34–35.

47. Moliné, p. 152.

48. Aristotle, 5.8.

49. Aquinas, 2-2.59.3.

50. Aquinas, 2-2.59.3.

51. *Catechism of the Catholic Church*, no. 387.

52. *Catechism of the Catholic Church*, no. 408.

53. Victor Hugo, *The Works of Victor Hugo*, vol. 11, *Les Misérables* (New York: Kelmscott Society, 1887), 23.

54. "Victor Hugo: Quotes: Quotable Quote," Goodreads, accessed February 11, 2022, *http://www.goodreads.com/quotes/18929-he-who-opens-a-school-door-closes-a-prison*.

55. Aquinas, 2-2.62.1–7.

56. Aquinas, 2-2.62.2.

57. Moliné, p. 182.

58. *Catechism of the Catholic Church*, no. 2258.

59. "Declaration of Independence: A Transcription," National Archives, The U.S. National Archives and Records Administration, accessed February 11, 2022, *https://www.archives.gov/founding-docs/declaration-transcript*.

60. Moliné, p. 155.

61. *Catechism of the Catholic Church*, nos. 2259–2261.

62. Aquinas, 2-2.64.6.

63. *Catechism of the Catholic Church*, no. 2297.

64. *Catechism of the Catholic Church*, nos. 2270–2275.

65. *Catechism of the Catholic Church*, nos. 2263–2265.

66. *Catechism of the Catholic Church*, nos. 2266–2267.

67. Moliné, p. 156.

68. Aquinas, 2-2.64.5.

69. Moliné, p. 160.

70. St. Paul VI, Pastoral Constitution on the Church in the Modern World *Gaudium et Spes* (December 7, 1965), no. 80. Vatican website: *www.vatican.va*.

71. *Catechism of the Catholic Church*, no. 2356.

72. Richard M. Doerflinger, "Human Embryo Research is Illegal, Immoral, and Unnecessary," United States Conference of Catholic Bishops, July 18, 2001, *https://www.usccb.org/issues-and-action/human-life-and-dignity/stem-cell-research/human-embryo-research-is-illegal-immoral-and-unnecessary*.

73. Congregation for the Doctrine of the Faith, Instruction on Respect for Human Life *Donum Vitae* (February 22, 1987), Introduction, nos. 4–5. Vatican website: *www.vatican.va*.

74. *Catechism of the Catholic Church*, no. 2296.

75. St. John Paul II, *Evangelium Vitae*, no. 86.

76. Rodríguez Luño, pp. 83–84.

77. *Catechism of the Catholic Church*, no. 2479.

78. Aquinas, 2-2.73.1.

79. Aquinas, 2-2.73.1–4.

80. Rodríguez Luño, p. 69.

81. Moliné, pp. 165–166.

82. Moliné, p. 166.

83. Aquinas, 2-2.74.1–2.

84. Aquinas, 2-2.75.1–2.

85. Aquinas, 2-2.76.1–2.

86. *Catechism of the Catholic Church*, no. 2476.

87. Aquinas, 2-2.98.1.

88. Moliné, p. 166.

89. Fr. Kenneth Baker, SJ, "Calumny and Detraction," Catholic Education Resource Center, accessed February 14, 2022, *https://www.catholiceducation. org/en/culture/catholic-contributions/calumny-and-detraction.html*.

90. *Catechism of the Catholic Church*, no. 2487.

91. "Defamation, Slander, and Libel," NOLO, accessed February 14, 2022, *https://www.nolo.com/legal-encyclopedia/defamation-slander-libel*.

92. Andrew Belsey and Ruth Chadwick, eds., *Ethical Issues in Journalism and the Media* (New York: Routledge, 1992), p. xi.

93. *Compendium of the Social Doctrine of the Church*, no. 416.

94. Richard Keeble, "Journalism Ethics: Towards an Orwellian Critique?," in *Journalism: Critical Issues*, ed. Stuart Allen (New York: Open University Press, 2005), p. 55.

95. Catherine Mayer, "Tabloid Bites Man," *Time*, July 25, 2011, pp. 26–28.

96. International Catholic Union of the Press, "International Principles of Professional Ethics in Journalism," *New City* 24, no. 2 (February 1989).

97. *Catechism of the Catholic Church*, no. 2405; see nos. 2403–2405.

98. Aquinas, 2-2.66.2.

99. Moliné, pp. 174–175.

100. Moliné, p. 177.

101. Aquinas, 2-2.66.2–4, 9.

102. *Catechism of the Catholic Church*, no. 2409.

103. Aquinas, 2-2.66.7.

104. Rodríguez Luño, p. 79.

105. J. Stapleton, "Occult Compensation," in *The Catholic Encyclopedia* (New York: Robert Appleton, 1908; NewAdvent online version, Kevin Knight), *https://www.newadvent.org/cathen/04186a.htm*.

106. Burgaleta, p. 63.

107. Burgaleta, p. 64.

108. Moliné, p. 182.

109. *Catechism of the Catholic Church*, 2240.

110. Alan Rappeport, "Tax Cheats Cost the U.S. $1 Trillion per Year, I.R.S. Chief Says," *New York Times*, April 13, 2021, *https://www.nytimes.com/2021/04/13/business/irs-tax-gap.html*.

111. William G. Gale and Aaron Krupkin, "How Big is the Problem of Tax Evasion?," April 3, 2019, Econofact, *https://econofact.org/how-big-is-the-problem-of-tax-evasion*.

112. Moliné, p.146. See also *https://www.ewtn.com/catholicism/library/do-we-have-to-pay-taxes-if-the-money-is-used-to-support-abortion-11061; https://philosophynow.org/issues/90/The_Ethics_of_Taxation; and https://thomasofaquino.blogspot.com/2019/04/is-one-morally-obliged-to-pay-all-taxes.html?m=1*

113. Tax evasion on moral grounds is hardly justifiable in democratic societies, where the governments are duly elected. But "The citizen is obliged in conscience not to follow the directives of civil authorities when they are contrary to the demands of the moral order, to the fundamental rights of persons or the teachings of the Gospel. *Refusing obedience* to civil authorities, when their demands are contrary to those of an upright conscience, finds its justification in the distinction between serving God and serving the political community. "Render therefore to Caesar the things that are Caesar's, and to God the things that are God's." "We must obey God rather than men." (*Catechism of the Catholic Church*, no. 2242)

114. Moliné, p. 146.

115. Aurelio Fernández, *Moral Especial: Iniciación Teológica*, 2nd ed. (Madrid: Ediciones Rialp, 2004), pp. 189–190.

116. St. John Paul II, Address to Members of the Confédération Fiscale Européenne (November 7, 1980). Vatican website: *www.vatican.va*.

117. Bishop Thomas J. Olmsted, "The Virtue of Justice," Catholic Culture, accessed February 14, 2022, *https://www.catholicculture.org/culture/library/view.cfm?recnum=7750*.

118. Aquinas, 2-2.73.3.

119. St. John Paul II, Encyclical Letter on the Hundredth Anniversary of *Rerum Novarum Centesimus Annus* (May 1, 1991), no. 44. Vatican website: *www.vatican.va.*

120. Francis Beckwith and Gregory Koukl, *Relativism: Feet Firmly Planted in Mid-Air* (Grand Rapids: Baker, 2005).

121. Pieper, p. 104.

122. St. Thomas Aquinas, *Super Mattheum*, 5.1.2, as quoted in Luiz Sérgio Solimeo, "Mercy without Justice Is the Mother of Dissolution; Justice without Mercy is Cruelty," The American Society for the Defense of Tradition, Family and Property, June 2, 2011, *https://www.tfp.org/mercy-without-justice-is-the-mother-of-dissolution-justice-without-mercy-is-cruelty/#easy-footnote-3-27739.*

123. Matthew Lee Anderson, "Why Justice Is Not Enough," *First Things*, November 13, 2009, *https://www.firstthings.com/blogs/firstthoughts/2009/11/why-justice-is-not-enough.*

124. Aquinas, 2-2.80.1.

125. Aquinas, 2-2.101.1.

126. Aquinas, 2-2.80.1.

127. Aquinas, 2-2.57.1.

128. Aquinas, 2-2.101.1.

129. Aquinas, 2-2.101.1.

130. Aquinas, 2-2.104.1–6.

131. McManaman, p. 80.

132. Nonetheless, it is enough for a person to do what needs to be done to avoid breaking a vow of obedience in a case where he or she is bound by a *vow of obedience*. Material obedience suffices.

133. Aquinas, 2-2.102.2–3.

134. Pieper, pp. 109–110.

135. Pieper, pp. 109–110.

136. Aquinas, 2-2.103.2.

137. Regan, pp. 103-105.

138. Aquinas, 2-2.109.3.

139. McManaman, p. 33.

140. Moliné, p. 161.

141. James Socias and Aurelio Fernández, *Our Moral Life in Christ: A Basic Course on Moral Theology* (Chicago: Midwest Theological Forum, 1997), p. 339.

142. McManaman, p. 33.

143. *Catechism of the Catholic Church*, no. 2486.

144. Moliné, p. 160.

145. Aquinas, 2-2.106.4.

146. Aquinas, 2-2.114.1–2; see also O'Keefe, p. 40, and McManaman, p. 64.

147. Aristotle, 4.5.

148. Aquinas, 2-2.117; see also O'Keefe, p. 41.

149. Aristotle, 4.1 and Aquinas, 2-2.117.2.

150. Aquinas, 2-2.117.2.

151. Aquinas, 2-2.117.6.

152. Aquinas, 2-2.120.1–2; see also O'Keefe, p. 42.

153. O'Keefe, p. 42.

154. Aquinas, 2-2.108.1–4; see also O'Keefe, p. 38.

155. McManaman, p. 56.

156. McManaman, pp. 56–57. See also O'Keefe, pp. 38–39.

157. Jacques Philippe, *The Eight Doors of the Kingdom: Meditations on the Beatitudes* (New York: Scepter, 2018), pp. 124–126.

158. St. Paul VI, *Gaudium et Spes*, no. 26.

159. Aquinas, 1-2.91.2.

160. Cessario, chap. 5.2, ebook version.

161. Adam Taylor, "What Does Social Justice Really Mean?," World Vision, February 20, 2012, *https://www.worldvision.org/blog/social-justice-really-mean*.

162. St. John Paul II, Encyclical Letter *Dives in Misericordia* (November 30, 1980), no. 12. Vatican website: *www.vatican.va*.

163. St. John Paul II, *Memory & Identity: Personal Reflections* (London: Weidenfeld and Nicolson, 2005), pp. 179–180.

164. Escrivá, no. 172.

CHAPTER THREE The Virtue of Fortitude

1. Eleanor Roosevelt, *You Learn by Living* (Louisville, KY: Westminster John Knox, 1960), pp. 29–30.

2. *Catechism of the Catholic Church*, no. 1808.

3. Aquinas, 2-2.123.1.

4. Aquinas, 2-2.123.1.

5. Pinsent, p. 41.

6. Peter Kreeft, *Back to Virtue* (San Francisco: Ignatius, 1992), p. 68.

7. Sensitive passion that is aroused when its movement toward a sensible good is impeded; its object is the difficult or arduous good.

8. Aquinas, 2-2.123.2.

9. Aristotle, *Nicomachean Ethics*, 3.6.

10. Timpe and Boyd, p. 83.

11. Andrés Humberto León, *Virtudes, Valores y Sentimientos* (Madrid, Spain: Editorial San Pablo, 2013); see the chapter on *Las Virtudes Cardinales*.

12. Pieper, p. 117.

13. Mattison III, p. 186.

14. Aquinas, 2-2.125.1.

15. Romano Guardini, *Learning the Virtues that Lead You to God* (Manchester, NH: Sophia Institute Press, 1998), pp. 99–101.

16. Aquinas, 2-2.139.1.

17. Bennett, p. 476.

18. Mattison III, p. 182.

19. We tend to extol more those who actually perish than those who survive (even if all of them are truly heroic) only because of the former's tragic end and dramatic effect.

20. Pieper, p. 122.

21. Aquinas, 2-2-.123.12.

22. Paul VI, *Gaudium et Spes*, no. 17.

23. Pieper, p. 125.

24. Aquinas, 2-2.125.2.

25. Pinckaers, p. 455.

26. Guardini, p. 102.

27. Regan, p. 109.

28. Aquinas, 2-2.123.6.

29. Aquinas, 2-2.123.3.

30. Victor Frankl, *Man's Search for Meaning* (New York: Pocket, 1963), pp. 106–107.

31. Aquinas, 2-2.158.1.

32. Regan, p. 106.

33. Aquinas, 2-2.123.10.

34. Pieper, p. 117.

35. Aquinas, 2-2.123.4.

36. Aquinas, 2-2.124.3.

37. Rickaby, p. 43.

38. Mark Shea, "St. Thomas More," Catholic Education Resource Center, accessed February 20, 2022, *https://www.catholiceducation.org/en/faith-and-character/faith-and-character/st-thomas-more.html.*

39. Aquinas, 2-2.123.8.

40. Pinsent, p. 50.

41. Escrivá, no. 77.

42. William Shakespeare, *Julius Caesar*, act 2, scene 2.

43. McManaman, p. 101.

44. Commit oneself irrevocably. In 49 BC, Julius Caesar crossed the Rubicon River that divided Italy and Gaul, leading a legion of soldiers to defy Roman law, thus starting a civil war that ultimately left him the undisputed ruler of the Roman world.

45. McManaman, pp. 99–100.

46. Aquinas, 2-2.126.2.

47. O'Keefe, p. 55.

48. Aquinas, 2-2.127.2.

49. Pieper, p. 124.

50. Pieper, p. 126.

51. Aquinas, 2-2.128.1; see also Timpe and Boyd, p. 84.

52. Aquinas, 2-2.129.1–8; see also McManaman, pp. 102–104.

53. Aquinas, 2-2.133.2.

54. O'Keefe, p. 61.

55. Aquinas, 2-2.132.1.

56. Aquinas, 2-2.132.5.

57. Aquinas, 2-2.131.1–2.

58. Aquinas, 2-2.134.3.

59. Aquinas, 2-2.134.3.

60. Aquinas, 2-2.134.3.

61. McManaman, p. 108.

62. Fernandez, p. 264.

63. Aquinas, 2-2.135.3.

64. O'Keefe, p. 63.

65. Cambridge Dictionry, s.v. "patience," accessed January 25, 2022, *https:// dictionary.cambridge.org/us/dictionary/english/patience.*

66. Aquinas, 2-2.136.4.

67. Rissa Singson-Kawpeng, *Confessions of an Impatient Bride* (Quezon City, Philippines: Shepherd's Voice, 2009), p. 8.

68. Aquinas, 2-2.136.5.

69. McManaman, p. 109.

70. Aquinas, 2-2.137.1.

71. Escrivá, no. 55.

72. Perseverance takes precedence over constancy because the difficulty aris-ing from the prolonged effort is more intrinsic to the virtue than that which is caused by external hindrances; see Aquinas, 2-2.137.3.

73. E. Allison Peers, trans. & ed., *The Complete Works of Saint Teresa of Jesus,* vol. 2 (London: Sheed and Ward, 1946), p. 89.

74. McManaman, p. 110.

75. Marcus Tullius Cicero, "Treatise on Rhetorical Invention" in *The Orations of Marcus Tullius Cicero,* vol. 4 (Bern, Switzerland: University of Bern, 1851), p. 375, *https://www.google.com/books/edition/Cicero_Orations/p_OWxrLu7 CcC?hl=en&gbpv=0.*

76. Escrivá, no. 57.

77. St. John Paul II, Encyclical Letter on Human Work *Laborem Exercens* (September 14, 1981), nos. 4–5, 9. Vatican website: *www.vatican.va.*

78. Isaacs, pp. 57–58.

79. Joseph De Torre, *Work, Culture, Liberation: The Social Teaching of the Church* (Quezon City, Philippines: Vera Reyes, 1985) p. 48.

80. Aquinas, 2-2.35.1.

81. Cardinal Stefan Wyszyński, *Work* (Chicago: Scepter, 1960), pp. 96–103.

82. Aquinas, 2-2.139.1.

83. Aquinas, 2-2.139.1.

84. Pinckaers, p. 455.

85. Aquinas, 2-2.124.2, as quoted in *The Summa Theologiae of St. Thomas Aquinas,* 2nd ed, *https://www.newadvent.org/summa/3124.htm#article2.*

86. Pieper, p. 141.

87. Francis, General Audience, May 14, 2014. Vatican website: *www.vatican.va*.

CHAPTER FOUR The Virtue Of Temperance

1. Regan, p. 119.

2. Burgaleta, p. 109.

3. Aquinas, 2-2.141.4.

4. Burgaleta, p. 110–111.

5. Pieper, p. 150.

6. O'Keefe, p. 71.

7. Aquinas, 2-2.31.5.

8. Aquinas, 2-2.141.7.

9. Insofar as they have any phenomenal consciousness.

10. *Catechism of the Catholic Church*, no. 356.

11. Aquinas, 2-2.23.4.

12. Seneca, *Seneca's Morals, by Way of Abstract*, rev. ed., trans. and ed. Roger L'Estrange and Lucius V. Bierce (Cleveland, OH: A. B., 1855), p. 129.

13. Fernandez, pp. 269–270.

14. Burgaleta, p. 113.

15. *Catechism of the Catholic Church*, no. 1809.

16. Linda Kavelin Popov, *The Family Virtues Guide* (New York: Penguin, 1997), p. 185.

17. Pieper, pp. 148–149.

18. Burgaleta, p. 110.

19. Mattison III, p. 87.

20. Aquinas, 2-2.33.3–4.

21. Mattison III, pp. 84–85.

22. Aquinas, 2-2.142.1–4.

23. Aquinas, 2-2.142.1.

24. Aquinas, 2-2.142.2.

25. Aquinas, 2-2.143.1; see also Regan, pp. 130–131.

26. Aquinas, 2-2.144.1–4.

27. O'Keefe, p. 74.

28. Aquinas, 2-2.145.1–4.

29. Aquinas, 2-2.145.2.

30. O'Keefe, pp. 75–76.

31. Regan, p. 135.

32. Aquinas, 2-2.146.1–2.

33. O'Keefe, p. 79.

34. Aquinas, 2-2.147.1.

35. Aquinas, 2-2.147.1 and 3.

36. Aquinas, 2-2.148.1–4.

37. Aquinas, 2-2.148.4.

38. Mark Shea, "St. Thomas More," Catholic Education Resource Center, accessed February 20, 2022, *https://www.catholiceducation.org/en/faith-and-character/faith-and-character/st-thomas-more.html*.

39. Timpe and Boyd, pp. 141–142.

40. As quoted in Francine Prose, *The Seven Deadly Sins: Gluttony* (New York: Oxford University Press, 2003), p. 19.

41. Aquinas, 2-2.149.1–4.

42. Aquinas, 2-2.150.1–4.

43. Rickaby, pp. 30–31.

44. Burgaleta, p. 118.

45. Aquinas, 2-2.151.1–4.

46. Aristotle, 3.12.

47. Pieper, pp. 153–154.

48. *Catechism of the Catholic Church*, no. 2337.

49. St. John Paul II, General Audience, January 9, 1980. Vatican website: *www.vatican.va*.

50. Pontifical Council for the Family, *The Truth and Meaning of Human Sexuality: Guidelines for Education within the Family* (December 8, 1995), nos. 10–11. Vatican website: *www.vatican.va*.

51. St. Augustine, *De Civitatis Dei*, 14, 18.

52. Carlos Zubieta, *Tras Las Ideas: Compendio de Historia de la Filosofía*, (Pamplona, Spain: EUNSA, 1996), pp. 219–224.

53. Peter Kreeft, "*The Pillars of Unbelief—Sigmund Freud*," Catholic Education Resource Center (CERC), in *catholiceducation.org*.

54. St. Paul VI, Encyclical Letter on the Celibacy of the Priest *Sacerdotalis Caelibatus* (June 24, 1967), no. 53. Vatican website: *www.vatican.va*.

55. Allan Bloom, *The Closing of the American Mind* (New York: Simon and Schuster, 1987), p. 98.

56. Aquinas, 2-2.153.1–5.

57. Aquinas, 2-2.153.5.

58. Aquinas, 2-2.155.1–4.

59. Aquinas, 2-2.152.3.

60. McManaman, p. 126.

61. Aristotle, 4.8.

62. O'Keefe, p. 81.

63. Aquinas, 2-2.156.1–4.

64. Aquinas, 2-2.161.1–6.

65. Aquinas, 2-2.161.5.

66. Jim Collins, *Good to Great* (New York: Harper Collins, 2001), p. 27.

67. McManaman, pp. 135–136.

68. Donald De Marco, *Heart of Virtue* (San Francisco: Ignatius, 1996), pp. 117–118.

69. McManaman, p. 135.

70. Aquinas, 2-2.161.3.

71. Aquinas, 2-2.162.1–8.

72. Aquinas, 2-2.162.6.

73. Pieper, p. 191.

74. McManaman, pp. 135–136.

75. As quoted in Robert Furey, *So I'm Not Perfect: A Psychology of Humility* (New York: St. Paul, 1986; Philippine Edition: Makati: St. Paul, 1991), p. 76.

76. Escrivá, no. 100.

77. Aquinas, 2-2.157.1–4.

78. Adolphe Tanquerey, *The Spiritual Life: A Treatise on Ascetical and Mystical Theology*, trans. Herman Branderis (Tournai, Belgium: Society of St. John the Evangelist, 1930), p. 1156.

79. Aquinas, 2-2.158.1–8.

80. Aristotle, 4.5.

81. Pieper, p. 195.

82. Philippe, pp. 105–106.

83. Pieper, pp. 195–196.

84. Aquinas, 2-2.157.1–4.

85. O'Keefe, p. 83.

86. Aquinas, 2-2.157.1–4; 159.1–2.

87. Aquinas, 2-2.160.1–2.

88. *Catechism of the Catholic Church*, no. 2521.

89. Bittle, p. 264.

90. Aquinas, 2-2.145.4.

91. Aquinas, 2-2.169.1–2.

92. Pius XII, Address to a Congress of the Latin Union of High Fashion (November 8, 1957), as quoted in "Moral Problems in Fashion Design," e-catholic2000, accessed January 27, 2022, *https://www.ecatholic2000.com/cts/untitled-295.shtml*.

93. Aquinas, 2-2.169.2.

94. *Catechism of the Catholic Church*, no. 2523.

95. *Catechism of the Catholic Church*, no. 2524.

96. Aquinas, 2-2.166.1–2.

97. Aquinas, 2-2.167.1.

98. Pieper, p. 200.

99. Aquinas, 2-2.168.2.

100. Aristotle, 4.8.

101. Aquinas, 2-2.152.1–5.

102. St. Josemaría Escrivá, *Conversations with Josemaría Escrivá* (New York: Scepter, 2007), no. 91.

103. Pieper, p. 178.

104. Aquinas, 2-2.143.

105. Aquinas, 2-2.118.3.

106. Aquinas, 2-2.118.7–8.

107. Javier Echevarría, *Itinerarios de Vida Cristiana* (Barcelona: Editorial Planeta, 2001), pp. 234–235.

108. O'Keefe, p. 92.

109. "Mortification," *The Catholic Encyclopedia*, vol. 10 (New York: Robert Appleton, 1911; Kevin Knight, 2022), *https://www.newadvent.org/cathen/10578b.htm*.

110. Escrivá, *Conversations*, no. 84.